Christian Counseling Handbook
For The 21st Century

Christian Counseling Handbook
For The 21st Century

By
William Perry, Th.D., Ph.D.

Endorsement:

Dr. William Perry is a gifted writer, preacher and servant of the Lord Jesus. He has spent many years of his life training and studying the scriptures. As a pastor, theologian and Christian Coach and Christian Counselor Dr. Perry has been a help and a blessing to many who have sought spiritual direction from the Bible.

Dr. Glenn Mollette
President of Newburgh Theological Seminary and College of the Bible.
Newburgh, Indiana
2016

Copyright (c) Dr. William Perry

ISBN: 978-0-9909250-1-9

Books may be ordered at Amazon.com or most any book dealer. Ask your local bookstore to order this book.

All rights reserved. No portion of this book may be reproduced, stored in a retrieval system, or transmitted in any form or by any means electronic, mechanical, photocopy, recording, or any other except for brief quotations in printed reviews, without the prior written permission of the publisher.

Newburgh Press
Newburgh, Indiana

Printed in the United States of America

ACKNOWLEDGEMENTS

I would like to thank my sons Jim and Eric, and daughter Jennifer, who greatly encouraged me, in finishing this book for publication, in order to share my years of experience with the world. I want to thank Pastor Lester DeGroot, who lovingly led me to my Lord and Savior, where I was Gloriously saved. Pastor John Whitaker and his wife Laverne for suppling friendship and encouragement at a time it was really needed. Dr. Glenn Mollette and his wife Carole, the staff of Newburg Seminary and College of the Bible and Newburgh Press for their continued support with this endeavor. Drs. Richard and Phyllis Arno, of the National Christian Counselors Association, for their assistance. And thanks to my wonderful wife Kathy, for her encouragement, guidance patience, suggestions, and continued assistance, without her this endeavor would never have gotten off the ground. I also want to thank MaLinda Wilhite for her hard work in proof reading, and getting the manuscript ready for publishing. Thanks also, to Brian Halley, for his creative abilities in designing a very attractive book cover. At this point, I pray I will never forget to give thanks to my wonderful Lord and Savor Jesus Christ for saving me, for guiding me, calling me to be a small part of His Work in this world.

Table of Contents

Acknowledgments VI
Introduction to Principles of Christian Counseling. 1
Chapter
    I. The Christian Approach to Counseling 2
    II. Presuppositions and Methodology. 7
    III. Creation Therapy. 9
    IV. Technique 12
Conclusion. 15
Introduction to Depression Counseling 17
    V. Categories of Depression. 19
    VI. Causes of Depression 20
    VII. The Bible and Depression 25
    VIII. Therapy for Depression 27
    IX. Assessment of Depression. 29
    X. Counseling/Treatment of Depression 32
Conclusion. 35
Intruduction to Marriage and Family Counseling. 37
    XI. Developing the Client Relationship 38
    XII. Teaching 46
    XIII. Therapy Process. 48
    XIV. Case Management. 55
    XV. The Bible and the Family 58
Conclusion. 62
Introduction To General Counseling 65
    XVI. The Time for a Change 67
    XVII. Types of Models 69
Conclusion. 79
Introduction to Legal and Ethical Practice 80
    XVIII. Perspective on Ethical Practice 81
    XIX. Therapy Legal Regulations 85
    XX. Ethical Conflicts 92
    XXI. Ethical Principles and Individual Conduct. 97

    XXII. Family Law 99
    XXIII. Rights of Institutionalized Patients 103
    XXIV. Professional Responsibilities and Liabilities. 106
Conclusion. 108
Introduction to Children and Adolescence 110
    XXV. The Multi-Method Approach 111
    XXVI. Planning Family Treatment and Orientation. 114
    XXVII. Assessing Children's Problems 115
    XXVIII. Changing Behavior 117
    XXIX. Helping Children Cope 118
    XXX. Using Games and Activities 120
    XXXI. Assigning New Behaviors 125
    XXXII. The Bible and Adolescence 130
Conclusion. 131
Introduction To Counseling into the Next Century 133
    XXXIII. Counselinginto the Next Century 134
Bibliography 136
End Notes 138

Introduction:
The Principles of Christian Counseling

For some time now it has been apparent that the need exists for a counseling model based on the presupposition that man is a created spirit being, created by God, with a soul and lives in a body.

In years past, in the early establishment of Christianity, the Church was solely responsible for the counseling of God's people. But because of the perception that the Christian community is not qualified to counsel its people, the humanists have largely taken over the responsibility of counseling.

Humanists believe that the Christian community does not have any real solutions to human problems, i.e. anxiety, abnormal stress, etc. In reality, no one is better qualified to counsel than those who know and understand man's unique position in the plan of creation and realize the place which God has for man in eternity.

> In most cases, the Christian community has simply taken the therapeutic methods developed by the secular community and applied them with a Biblical approach. But we as Christian counselors must approach counseling with the assumption that God has created man in his image, and through His Word, the Bible, can give much insight into the mind of man.

Chapter 1
The Christian Approach

The field of Christian counseling utilizes a variety of therapeutic approaches, as is true in secular psychology and psychiatry. In spite of a basic unity derived from the oneness in Christ and their acceptance of the Bible as an absolute standard, Christian counselors differ from each other in personality, the training they have received, their experience, the setting in which they practice, and the kinds of counselees who come to them for help. All of those factors influence one's approach to counseling.[1]

In essence, the counseling process can be understood as a three-part ministry or service to the counselee offered by the counselor. Basically, a counselor performs the following functions:

Let the counselee ventilate. (Listen to the counselee).

Help the counselee gain insight.

Help the counselee formulate a specific plan of action.

Simply talking to another person often relieves one's problems. True friendship is built when one person listens to another and shows genuine concern.

Caring, although intangible, is readily sensed by people, particularly those with problems. People tend to gravitate toward those individuals who are warm, understanding, accepting, personal and willing to listen. Unless counselees develop a caring relationship with a counselor, they are seldom motivated to change. Listening is one of the best ways to express concern or caring.

Good listening techniques can be learned. According to Drs. Meier, Minirth, and Winchern, when working with two people at once, try to talk to only one person at a time and not engage in two conversations. It is important to avoid interrupting any person who is speaking. A good listener does not tune in to only part of the conversation, argue mentally while the other person is talking, and jump to conclusions before that person finishes. Care should be taken not to appear restless or to convey disinterest by one's facial expressions. A warm smile, eye contact, and interest shown by every movement, according to Drs. Meier, Minirth, and Winchern are the marks of a good listener. Counselors must not let their own biases affect therapy. Counselees can usually tell if they are being "pigeonholed" mentally or labeled by a counselor as they speak, especially if the counselor uses emotionally charged words in response. Also, it is wise for a listener to avoid making notes unless he or she is willing to share them.

The key to counseling is to help a counselee gain insight. Once people gain insight into the true nature of their problem, much of the problem may resolve. A counselor can often help by maintaining a balance between focus on the past and attention to the present, by clarifying the difference between feelings and behavior, and by using directive and nondirective techniques appropriately.

In counseling today the pendulum seems to be swinging from focusing on the past to focusing on the present. One extreme position has always blamed the past for present problems; the other has avoided the past and focused counseling almost entirely on the present. For example, reality therapy emphasizes that the past is past and can never be changed. In general, past experiences should not be used as excuses to avoid present responsibilities. Christian counseling endeavors to deal with present behavior; but sometimes it is appropriate to do something about unresolved issues from the past. Overall, taking a balanced view tends to work best.

For a Christian of course, the past is forgiven. "If we confess our sins, He is faithful and just and will forgive us our sins and purify us from all unrighteousness." (1 John 1:9) "...But one thing I do: Forgetting what is behind and straining toward what is ahead, I press on toward the goal to win the prize for which God has called me heavenward in Christ Jesus." (Philippians 3:13-14) Although the past is forgiven by God, guilt may still haunt an individual consciously or subconsciously, and hence must be dealt with in counseling.

Although one extreme in counseling focuses entirely on feelings and another entirely on behavior, Christian counseling must treat both as important. It is important to let counselees ventilate and talk out their feelings. This helps them cope with the internalized anger that causes depression and helps to bring their anxiety from the subconscious to the conscious, where it can be dealt with appropriately. It also helps counselees feel that the counselor cares for them and understands them. The Christian counselor must move beyond attention to feelings, however, to deal with behavior. After all, people in a depressed state have little direct control over their behavior: Troubled individuals generally benefit from developing new interest and activities.

It is often possible to change feelings by changing behavior. Memories and feelings from the past recorded in the brain (in the subconscious) can be replayed later. One way to change feelings is to reprogram the mind by studying the Scriptures: "Do not conform to the pattern of this world, but be transformed by the renewing of your mind. Then you will be able to test and approve what God's will is—His good, pleasing and perfect will." (Romans 12:2)

A counselor can help individuals gain insight into their problems by using the proper counseling technique with the proper attitude and at the proper time.

Two broad divisions of counseling are directive and nondirective. Conventional psychiatry is essentially nondirective. The therapist does not attempt to tell patients what they should do, but rather operates on the principle that once patients understand why things have gone wrong, they will change as insight supposedly leads to changed behavior. Directive counseling, on the other hand, attempts to teach patients better ways to fulfill their needs. If counselors are too directive they defeat their own purpose, because only decisions that are personal convictions will last. But counseling that is not sufficiently directive also confuses counselees, since they are left with too few guidelines to follow.

Christian counseling generally uses an approach called 'indirect – directive". The Christian counselor should be able to recognize an individual's problem and then guide him or her in achieving it. Because the Bible serves as the standard of authority, Christian counseling is directive. Its goals are to help counselees solve their problems in accordance with the will of God and to help them grow spiritually. Yet the preferred approach is indirect because the counselor generally uses indirect techniques (questions, suggestive statements, listening) to help the counselee reach appropriate decisions. The Christian counselor thus uses indirect techniques for a directed end. Jesus Christ was directive at times and nondirective at other times, as in His use of parables. He helped others obtain valuable insights through both statements and questions. His statements were stern and rebuking at times but kind and gentle at other times. The Gospel of Mark records approximately twenty questions asked by Christ. Some of those questions were matter-of-fact, intending to teach others or help them gain insight, but at least five of them were rebuking in nature (three directed at the Pharisees and two at the disciples). Questions often force people to think and reach their own conclusions and are valuable tools to an experienced counselor.

Balance is the key to spiritual and emotional maturity: It is also the key to successful Christian counseling. Jesus Christ demonstrated how to be both direct and indirect in helping people gain insight (see John 3), how to focus on the present without excluding the past (see John 4), and how to major on spiritual aspects without neglecting the physical and psychological aspects (see John 5).

Emotional and spiritual balance was also reflected in the apostle Paul's counseling. One passage in particular illustrates his balanced approach: "And we urge you, brothers, warn those who are idle, encourage the timid, help the weak, be patient with everyone" (1 Thessalonians 5:14).[2]

Chapter II
Presuppositions and Methodology

In considering the methodology of counseling, it is important first to speak of the place and importance of methodology, then to compare and contrast Biblical methods with some of those that are employed by others. The issue at stake is: what methods may Christians use in counseling? Counseling methodology is so integrally related to counseling philosophy that, in the words of Perry London, who makes no pretense of being a Christian, if you want to understand the core ideas of a system, "the analysis of techniques serves understanding more than any other possible approach to this discipline."[3] Yet Baker, writing in a conservative Christian magazine, naively speaks of the "moral neutrality" of methodology or techniques.[4] Thereby, he places an aspect of this outside of the concern of God.

The issue, to be sure, takes one form when speaking about the techniques of mechanics who service an automobile and another when discussing the techniques of the repairman who seeks to change the life and values of another human being. The values involved in the methodology of auto mechanics are more indirectly related to methodology. Some excuse for failing to see the impossibility of neutrality with reference to the former might be understandable, but how can one speak of "moral neutrality" with reference to the control and manipulation of men? Surely the crucial importance of methodology, therefore, may not be by-passed.

Counseling methodology, as London rightly has said, is "a moral question that is always answered by the therapist in practice."[5] Indeed, it could not be otherwise. What we do to another person and how we do it is tightly bound up with what we believe about that person. If, with Skinner, we assume that a man is only another animal, we shall seek to train him as we would train our dogs and do it precisely the same way. In other words, we shall adopt methods that are appropriate to training animals. On Skinner's methods, we treat man as if he were only an animal. On Skinner's presuppositions, methods used in training a man and a rat will differ only insofar as the man and the contingencies necessary to control him may be considered more complex. There will be no basic differences. If we acknowledge the existence of the image of God in man, however, this very belief will demand a methodology discrete from that which is used in training a dog. Dogs, for instance, may not be called to repentance and faith in Jesus Christ; neither may they be converted and persuaded by the Spirit of God to live according to His Word. But according to Christian presupposition a man may, indeed must. Christian methodology, therefore, is conditioned radically by Christian beliefs. Christians insist that counseling methodology necessarily must grow out of and always be appropriate to the Biblical view of God, man, and creation.

Chapter III
Creation Therapy

One of the new models of Christian Counseling is Creation Therapy. Creation therapy is based on the theory of temperament (understanding of the inner man) and uses this knowledge to help the counselee understand himself. Therefore, it allows us to be the best that God has created us to be by meeting the needs of temperament equally and Scripturally. Although this therapeutic method is a fairly new concept (developed in 1983), by Richard G. Arno, Ph.D. and Phyllis J. Arno, Ph.D., it appears to have been very successful.[6]

The theory teaches that man is a spiritual being created by God with a precise order and balance of body, soul and spirit. The spirit encompasses our temperament and our heart is the binding, blending, and balancing agent within our temperament. The theory teaches that our temperament is placed within us by God while in our mother's womb and that this temperament will remain with us throughout our lives. The overlap of this temperament with the soul and spirit provides God's precise order within each of us. Creation therapy identifies the temperament needs in counselees and helps them find a balance in order to relieve the inner stress. This therapeutic procedure will help counselees reach their full potential within their environment and with the Lord.

Many scholars are of the opinion that any therapy based on this theory of temperament "types" individuals. That is to say, it is narrow in scope and has "little boxes" in which it places people. According to Dr. Richard Gene Arno and Dr. Phyllis Jean Arno, nothing could be farther from the truth because there are thousands of different temperament blends. Creation therapy focuses on the uniqueness of each individual, not the reverse.[7]

In Creation therapy, the counselee's temperament needs must be determined. With this information his needs can be pinpointed and the ones that are currently causing him/her problems can be identified. In other words, his/her current problems are probably being caused by meeting a temperament need in an ungodly way. This way must be identified and replaced with a godly method.

"For the word of God is alive and active. Sharper than any double-edged sword, it penetrates even to dividing soul and spirit, joints and marrow; it judges the thoughts and attitudes of the heart." (Hebrews 4:12)[8]

"May God himself, the God of peace, sanctify you through and through. May your whole spirit, soul and body be kept blameless at the coming of our Lord Jesus Christ." (1 Thessalonians 5:23).[9]

As we believe we are all spiritual beings, who possess a soul and live in a body. It is quite possible to develop or educate a human mind, and also to develop a human body. It must also be possible to develop a human spirit. God would not give man the capacity for developing the mind and body without including man's spirit, or else man would not have been created a spiritual being.

Even the scientific/medical community recognizes this in terms of a therapeutic classification. According to Taber's Cyclopedic Medical Dictionary, F.A. Davis Company, Philadelphia, PA, 1968, "spiritual therapy is the application of spiritual knowledge in the treatment of all mental and physical disorders, based upon the assumption that man is a spiritual being living in a spiritual universe; that in proportion to his acceptance of this idea, and in proportion to his success in demonstrating it, he may control his body and the material elements in harmony with a Divine plan." [10]

It is the spirit of man that contacts God. We do not contact God with our physical senses. It is the spiritual part of man that contacts God and experiences ultimate reality in fellowship with Him. Just like

Adam in the Garden of Eden, it is through this communication that man's heart is totally satisfied. The only way man can find this reality (peace, love, joy, satisfaction) is through the rebirth of the human spirit by accepting Jesus as Savior.

"Therefore, if any man be in Christ, he is a new creature; old things are passed away; behold, all things are become new." (2 Corinthians 5:17 KJV)[11]

Through identification of each individual's needs, and, teaching that individual how to meet these needs in godly ways, ways conducive to the Holy Scriptures, the individual is taught to develop his/her spirit. This is accomplished with a step-by-step therapeutic format based on the Word of God.

Chapter IV
Technique

With the presupposition and principles basic to Biblical counseling, and now, following forward with the practice of Biblical counseling, we must consider the processes in which techniques are employed. It seems that in the overall practice of counseling, it is necessary to address the matter of technique itself.

Christians sometimes have problems with the thought and very idea of using a technique. Such difficulties are not associated only with counseling, but also preaching, teaching, and many other areas in which acquisition and use of skills in the development of one's gifts, when they are required to be used to accomplish the required results, and as such, play a dominant part. It is very important for Christians to understand that problems concerning techniques are not really problems with technique itself, rather they arise from the use of technique apart from the power of the Holy Spirit. According to Jay Adams in his book, The Christian Counselor's Manual, the problem most frequently appears in two forms: (1) attempting to counsel in one's own strength without the spirit; (2) attempting to use techniques that are contrary to the principles recorded by the Spirit in the Scriptures. Some earnest Christians confuse the use of techniques with the abuse of techniques and, as a result, reject the study or use of techniques in total. This is a tragic mistake.[12] The Spirit does not place a premium on being careless or using sloppy technique when confronting or counseling others. We can see from reading the Scriptures that skillfulness is something to attempt achieving, as this is often emphasized. For example, Paul warned, "Be very careful, then, how you live..." (Ephesians 5:15)[13] "Be wise in the way you act toward outsiders;... Let your conversation be always full of grace, seasoned with salt, so that you may know how to answer everyone." (Colossians 4:5, 6)[14] All of those statements require us to focus primarily on technique, but technique properly under control of God the Holy Spirit. Paul, it appears, was concerned not only about what, but also about how.

Counseling is not a step-by-step process like preparing a meal or repairing a car, or putting together a cabinet. Each counselee is unique, with problems, attitudes, values, expectations, and experiences that are unlike any other. The counselor who has his own problems that he brings to the counseling session must approach each individual a little differently, and will soon discover that the course of counseling will vary quite a lot from person to person.

Gary Collins, Ph. D. in his book, Christian Counseling, pg. 29, gives us this information; "In every counseling relationship, it would appear that there are several steps, the first three of which may be repeated several times as problems are considered and reconsidered. These steps involve building and maintaining a relationship between counselor and counselee; exploring problems to clarify issues and determine how the problems can be handled; deciding on a course of action; stimulating the counselee to act; evaluating progress and deciding on subsequent actions; and terminating the counseling relationship by encouraging and guiding the counselee to launch out without the counselor's continuing help."[15]

On the surface, this all sounds pretty simple and to the point, but the process of counseling can be much more complicated and demanding than it might seem, and demand the limits of a counselor's time and energy.

One of the reasons for this is that the steps are seldom identified so clearly or easily as explained by Dr. Collins, as previously stated. For example, the first step of building a relationship is very important at the beginning when all parties might be nervous and apprehensive. However, once the relationship is underway, it must be maintained, so the counselor must never completely lose sight of this process. In counseling there tends to be a vacillation back and forth as problems become clearer, solutions are found, and you move the counseling toward termination.

The counselor should prepare for counseling largely by prayer for himself and for his patients/counselees. Prayer for the counselee may grow naturally out of preparation for the session, reading notes, going over the file, etc. This prayer will take the form of the counselee's needs, abilities to understand and grasp truth, follow directions and apply truths. Prayer will also request understanding of the Scriptures. When prayer grows out of, and, becomes a regular part of your mental process, intellectual consideration, both its content and fervor are likely to be much greater. Often God may use such prayer to help the counselor develop fruitful plans for the next session. There is a danger with prayer being abused. The counselor may start depending on prayer to directly change the situation. "...faith by itself, if it is not accompanied by action, is dead." (James 2:17)[16] The conclusion is most clear. Prayer and faith in God to answer that prayer is essential. "And without faith it is impossible to please God..." (Hebrews 11:6)[17] It is also essential to get personally involved and to use the gifts and talents God gave you, and your training as a counselor to teach the counselee to confidently stand on God's Word even in the midst of trials and temptations, and to learn to trust you, the counselor to be trustworthy in working toward solving the counselee's problems, with God's help.

Conclusion

The following is one of the most meaningful Biblical truths that we can use in Christian counseling; "Come unto me, all ye that labor and are heavy laden, and I will give you rest. Take my yoke upon you, and learn of me; for I am meek and lowly in heart; and ye shall find rest unto your souls. "For my yoke is easy, and my burden is light." (Matthew 11:28-30)[18] To understand how these verses play a part in Christian counseling, I want to draw some parallel lines for practical life today.

"Come unto me, all ye that are heavy laden and I will give you rest." (v.28) To the individual Christian, it does not mean that God will protect us from hard work. In the book of Genesis, God directed, or ordained that man should work hard, to "live by the sweat of his brow." To truly understand what this verse means, we must first understand what in the human condition causes a man to become exhausted spiritually, physically and emotionally.

A man becomes spiritually exhausted when he spends much of his life searching for God and trying to earn His love by following a long list of meaningless religious laws and useless rituals. He becomes spiritually weary when all of his efforts have been exhausted. Still he finds no peace in his soul, no joy in his life, and God is still a faraway and unattainable Being.

Next, a man will become exhausted when he neglects and pushes himself well beyond his physical endurance or when internal stress depletes his energy reserves.

Emotionally a man can become exhausted because exhaustion is the byproduct of a person doing his best to do the right things and obeying as best he can to all the rules, and yet internal stress leaves him without any means to withstand the stress of his environment.

Christ promised that we would receive rest from this exhaustion, and how we receive this rest is found in Matthew 11:29: "Take my yoke upon you and learn of me." The yoke that Christ speaks of in this verse is symbolic.

Yokes were made so the owner could steer the beast, but this yoke that was used was also made so the animal could work longer and more efficiently by tiring less under his heavy burdens. This mechanism was made of heavy wood, not padded as they are today. Therefore, they had to be measured to fit perfectly.

When we accept the perfectly fitting yoke of Christ that He has provided for us, rest, peace and joy are the results. Then we are able to learn of Christ. His Words and His ways free us from the stress and pressures that plague all of us.

When an individual is physically sick or exhausted, or emotionally stressed or strained, they are short-tempered, depressed, withdrawn and not pleasant to the people around them. They may be angry at and question God regarding His methods and motives. In this state, they may be hard to reach for Christ. They lack the strength to do any of the good works that God has given them to do, and they lack strength or willpower to withstand the persecution of Satan. This is a chain reaction that can occur, and this is likely to be the state, or condition of the counselee at the time the counselor first comes in contact with him.

Counseling must bring about change, and will work toward bringing the counselee to a self-discipline relationship, where he will be able to see the wisdom in extracting for himself, Scripture to help him with the decisions he has to make regarding his own life.

The wise counselor will use all of the resources that God has given him in his calling as a counselor for the service of the Lord to bring about this change.

Introduction to Depression Counseling

At some time in each of our lives we have had the experience of rejection. It may have come with a girlfriend in high school, a marriage proposal, college entrance application, missed promotions, a home loan that we didn't qualify for. We also have probably experienced other disappointments. Now think about the ways one might react to the rejection, or other disappointments. One might feel hurt, angry, or both. All would be "normal" reactions.

As we look into the Bible, we find that Jesus was rejected, and knows all about our disappointments. As Christians, we can go to Him when we feel rejected, and know that He will understand. Isaiah had prophesied that Jesus would be despised and rejected by men.[19] The people He came to save were the very ones who nailed Him to that well known wooden instrument of death.[20] Then, on the cross Jesus shouted to God in heaven, "My God, my God, why have you forsaken me?"[21] Even His Father had Jesus hang on the cross alone. Despite this rejection He encountered, He never abandoned His mission, never retaliated against those who scorned Him.

According to the writer of Hebrews, Jesus can sympathize with our weakness and pain and give us His grace to help when we're hurting. So when we're rejected, we can choose to let sin, and bitterness, anger, fear, doubt or loneliness bring on depression to dominate our life. But these negative emotions can destroy us; they can give Satan a foothold in our life. Or, when we're hurt, disappointed and rejected, we can go to God the Redeemer. He calls us to forgive, to love our enemies and pray for those who persecute us,[22] and these commands are good counsel. They can free us from the kind of bitterness that is a root cause of depression that kills our spirit and blocks our relationship with God and man. It's only when we adopt the attitude of responsibility for our actions and attitudes, and turn them to God with repentance that we can fully experience His healing. In this way God will be glorified, and we will experience freedom from the past and from the pain we have been feeling.

Chapter V
Categories of Depression

In their book, Introduction to Psychology & Counseling; a Christian prescriptive, Drs. Meier, Minirth and Wichern list five categories of depressive disorders. The least severe, clinical depression includes the sad effect, painful thinking, physical systems, and anxiety. If those systems disable the individual biologically and socially, the disorder is called depressive neurosis, which can be cured by professional psychotherapy. Depressed individuals who have considerable anxiety along with sad effect, painful thinking, and psychomotor retardation are said to have agitated depression, which is also curable. Depressed individuals who develop delusional thinking, or hallucinations, have a psychotic depression which is usually curable if caught early, although more difficult to treat. Psychotic depressions that worsen may become life-long schizophrenic disorders, which are at present improvable through therapy but nearly impossible to cure.[23]

We want at this time to mention the Manic-depressives. It is possible that bizarre behavior of persons who exhibit what has been called manic-depressives react as the result of various underlying causes. There is at the present no conclusive evidence that etiology is ever organic. However, the possibility that etiology or some such instance of behavior labeled "manic-depressive" as organic is held open.[24]

Chapter VI
Causes of Depression

Modern genetic research has produced some popular distortions. Some people blame everything on their "bad genes". Although our genetic make-up does have an enormous effect on our intellectual and emotional potentials, our degree of wisdom and happiness as adults is not predetermined genetically. As we consider the causes of depression, we can basically rule out genetics as a factor. Most human depression is the result of irresponsible behavior, our own irresponsible handling of anger and guilt. Some individuals are irresponsible because they choose to be, others are irresponsible because they lack knowledge. Most of us need to grow in knowledge of how to handle our own emotions responsibly and know how to use that knowledge.

Most human beings, however, hate to face up to their own responsibility, especially their emotional state. It is much easier to blame our woes on others, unfair treatment by the world, hypoglycemia, or "bad genes".

Pent-up anger is the root of nearly all clinical depression cases.[25] Investigators have identified a number of causes for depression, causes which, when understood, can facilitate counseling.

1. **Physical-Genetic Causes.** Depression often has a physical basis. Lack of sleep and improper diet are among the simplest physical causes. Others, like the effects of drugs, low blood sugar and other chemical malfunctioning, brain tumors, or glandular disorders, are more complicated. Then there is research which has stressed the importance of hypothalamus in producing depression. No matter how good one's philosophy, no matter how well adjusted one has been, and no matter how ideal the environment may be, when there is a loss of hypothalamic

energy, the person is depressed, feels helpless, and has no energy. Only a return of normal neurohormonal energy in the hypothalamus can affect a resolution of the depressive mood.[26] Although it is not conclusive, there is some evidence to show that severe depression may run in families. This has not led to the conclusion that some people innately may be more prone to depression than others.

2. **Background Causes.** Do childhood experiences lead to depression in later life? Some evidence would say "yes". Many years ago, a researcher named Rene Spitz published a study of children who had been separated from their parents and raised in an institution. Deprived of continuing warm human contact with an adult, these children showed apathy, poor health, and sadness, all indicative of depression which could continue into later life. In addition, depression is more likely when parents blatantly or subtly reject their children or when status-seeking families set unrealistically high standards which children are unable to meet. When standards are too high, failure becomes inevitable and the person becomes depressed as a reaction to the marked discrepancy between goals and achievements.[27] Such early experiences do not always lead to depression but they increase the likelihood of severe depression in later life.[28]

3. **Learned Helplessness.** A more recent theory maintains that depression comes when we encounter situations over which we have no control. When we learn that our actions are futile no matter how hard we try, that there is nothing we can do to relieve suffering, reach a goal or bring change, then depression is a common response. It comes when we feel helpless and give up trying. This might explain the prevalence of depression in the grieving person who can do nothing to bring back a loved one, for example, or in the student who is unable to relate to his peers

or succeed academically, or in the older person who is powerless to turn back the clock and restore lost physical capacities. When such people are able to control at least a portion of their environment, depression subsides and often disappears.[29]

4. **Negative thinking.** It takes almost no effort to slip into a pattern of negative thinking, seeing the dark side of life and overlooking the positive. But negative thinking can lead to depression and when the depressed person continues to think negatively, more intense depression results.

According to psychiatrist, Aaron Beck, depressed people show negative thinking in three areas. First, they view the world and life experiences negatively. Life is seen as a succession of burdens, obstacles, and defeats in a world which is "going down the drain". Second, many depressed people have a negative view of themselves. They feel deficient, inadequate, unworthy and incapable of performing adequately. This in turn can lead to self-blame and self-pity. Third, these people view the future in a negative way. Looking ahead they see continuing hardship, frustration, and hopelessness.[30]

Is such negative thinking a cause for depression or is it a result of depression? The answer is probably both. Because of past experiences or previous training we begin to think negatively. This leads to depression which can lead to more negative thinking.

Such negative thinking sometimes may be used to control others. If there are people who think everything is bleak, others try to "back them up". A comment, "I'm no good," often is an unconscious way of getting others to say, "Oh, no, you really are a fine person." Self-condemnation, therefore, becomes a way of manipulating others to give compliments. But such comments aren't really satisfying so the negative thinking and depression goes on. If you keep thinking negatively, you are less likely to be hurt or disappointed if some of your thinking comes true.

5. **Life Stress.** It is well known that the stresses of life stimulate depression, especially when these stresses involve a loss. Loss of an opportunity, a job, status, health, freedom, a contest, possessions or other valued objects can each lead to depression. Then there is the loss of people. Divorce, death, or prolonged separations are painful and known to be among the most effective depression-producing events in life.

6. **Anger.** The oldest, most common and, perhaps, most widely accepted explanation of depression is that it involves anger which turns inward against oneself. Many children are raised in homes and sent to schools where the expression of anger is not tolerated. Some attend churches where anger is condemned as sin. Other people become convinced that they shouldn't even feel angry so they deny hostile feelings when they do arise. A widow, for example, may be angry at her husband who died leaving her to raise the children alone, but such anger seems irrational and is sure to arouse guilt in the person who thinks such thoughts about the dead. A result, the anger is denied and kept within.

What happens then, when one gets frustrated, resentful and angry? If the anger is denied or pushed out of our minds, it festers "under cover" and eventually gets us down.

Perhaps most anger begins when we feel hurt, because of a disappointment or because of the actions of some other person. Instead of admitting this hurt, people mull it over, ponder what happened, and begin to get angry. The anger then builds and becomes so strong that it hides the hurt. If the anger is not admitted and expressed and dealt with, it then leads to revenge. This involves thoughts of hurting another person, either the one who caused the original hurt, or someone else who is nearby. Revenge sometimes leads to destructive violent actions, but this can get us into trouble, and violence is not acceptable, especially for a Christian. As a result, some people try to hide their feelings. This takes energy, which wears down the body so that the emotions eventually come to the surface in the form of psychosomatic symptoms. Others, consciously or unconsciously, condemn themselves for their attitudes and become depressed as a result. This depression may be a form of emotional self-punishment which sometimes even leads to suicide. It is easy to understand why such people feel that they are no good, guilty and unhappy. Some people use their depression as a subtle and socially acceptable way to both express anger and to get revenge.

7. **Guilt.** It is not difficult to understand why guilt can lead to depression. When a person feels that he or she has failed or has done something wrong, guilt arises and along with it comes self-condemnation, frustration, hopelessness and other systems of depression. Guilt and depression so often occur together that it is difficult to determine which comes first. Perhaps in most cases guilt comes before depression but at times depression will cause people to feel guilty. In either case a vicious cycle is set in motion.

Chapter VII
The Bible and Depression

The Bible does not actually mention depression, but a number of passages refer to depressive conditions. The Psalmist cried out a number of times with cries that imply depression. Consider the following Psalms, for example, 69, 89, and 102. These songs are of deep despair, but one can't help but notice that they are set in a context of hope. In Psalm 43, King David proclaims both depression and rejoicing:

> Why are you in despair, O my soul?
> And why are you disturbed within me?
> Hope in God, for I shall again praise Him.
> The help of my countenance, and my God. [31]

Elsewhere in the Bible it appears that Job, Moses, Jonah, Peter and the whole nation of Israel experienced depression.[32] Jeremiah the prophet wrote a whole book of lamentations. Elijah saw God's mighty power at work on Mt. Carmel, but when Jezebel threatened murder, Elijah fled to the wilderness where he plunged into despondency. He wanted to die and might have done so except for the treatment that came from an angel sent by God.[33]

Then there was Jesus in Gethsemane, where He was greatly distressed, an observation which is poignantly described in the words of the Amplified Bible: "He began to show grief and distress of mind and was deeply depressed. Then He said to them, My Soul is very sad and deeply grieved, so that I am almost dying of sorrow…"

Such examples, accompanied by numerous references to pain of grieving, show the realism that characterizes the Bible. But this realistic despair is contrasted with certain hope. Each of the believers who plunged into depression eventually came through and experienced a new and lasting joy.[34]

A basic step in overcoming depression for anyone is to accept Jesus Christ as personal Savior. Although Christians are not free from the problems, they have a source of strength in their relationship to Christ. "Believing in Christ" includes both understanding that Christ died for our sins and trusting Him for our own salvation. With Christ as our savior and brother and God as our heavenly Father, a tremendous resource for help is gained. One of the best ways to overcome depression is to daily commit one's life to the purpose of glorifying Christ.

Now may the God of hope fill you with all joy and peace in believing, that you may abound in hope by the power of the Holy Spirit. [35]

Chapter VIII
Therapy for Depression

When planning a therapy program, the identification and description of specific therapist tasks and strategies should alert and sensitize the therapist to activities necessary for the organization and planning of the therapy sessions. The presentation of specific techniques will provide the clinician with the appropriate tools to treat depressed individuals. It is clearly recognized that each case of depression will have its own unique features, circumstances, and complexities. A point of interest, the therapist is not often concerned with issues of why something happened, "why" questions tend to be unproductive and frequently lead to feelings of guilt and blame. Instead, the therapist attends to the sequence of interactions stimulated by an event. This principle maintains that one reason a family gets stuck, is that they become overly concerned with the content of their conflict, which often takes them down a dead-end road. A therapist can become too involved with the content of the arguments, and neglect the process of their interactions, and become absorbed into the family's pathology. This absorption occurrence may be indicated if the therapist finds himself in alliance with one family member or if he has experienced a particular situation with the same degree of emotional intensity as the family.

In addition to some general principles and strategies, the therapist also engages in specific tasks during the course of his involvement with a depressed patient and family. This process involves diagnosing the depression and assessing its functional role in the family. In addition to specific therapeutic tasks, the therapist also uses particular techniques and intervention strategies consistent with the orientation requirements.

The fundamental objectives of the therapist are twofold. First, the therapist must help the family to appreciate the importance of working together as a system to both understand the depression and alleviate it. In essence, the therapist must teach the family about systems and how they work. This aspect of therapy is particularly important given most people's tendency to conceptualize depression in linear and intrapsychic terms. If the therapist is to work effectively with a family, that family must be helped to expand its perception of the depression.

In working with individuals, there are two major goals that differentiate from working with families. First, the individual must understand the effect of his depression on those around him. Second, the therapist must try to attenuate the depressed person's increased accessibility to negative stimuli. A number of procedures are available to accomplish this objective, and interestingly, several of those techniques are already used routinely by cognitive and behavioral therapists in the treatment of depression, albeit with different underlying rationales. [36]

Chapter IX
Assesment of Depression

Consistent with the general description of depression, it is important that assessment of the depressed individual and of the marital dyad or family be performed with the degree of equal importance, and with the understanding that both are necessary precursors to an interpersonal system approach to treatment. Therefore, the individual assessment procedures for depression should include an evaluation of the immediate social environment of the depressed person. In this context, techniques used in interviewing families with a depressed member should be assessed and measured. In organizing the assessment session or sessions it is recommended that the therapist start by seeing either the marital dyad or the entire family, depending on the nature of the referral and the impact of the depression on the family. The assessment and therapeutic process begins from the family member's first telephone contact with the therapist during which the therapist should make explicit the ground rules for an interpersonal approach to therapy. In all probability, the single rule with the greatest initial impact on the contacting family member involves the decision regarding who is to be seen in therapy. Most often, the family member initiating the first contact with the therapist will define the problem as involving only one family member, or only one part of the family. At this point, the therapist must decide which family members are to be seen in the subsequent assessment sessions.

An exception to seeing at least the marital dyad in therapy involves cases in which an individual from an intact family contacts a therapist requesting intervention for personal depression, and despite the therapist's request, refuses to involve the spouse or children in the treatment process. The therapist must then make a decision regarding his willingness to work with this person alone. The decision to refrain from working with individuals in therapy because they refuse to involve the spouses or families in treatment is difficult for a therapist to make.

It might be well to emphasize that while the decision of who to see in the assessment sessions is important, it is not set in stone. In terms of logistics, while the therapist is interviewing the depressed individual alone, the spouse, and children are requested to complete a number of questionnaires in another room. When this interview is completed, the teams trade places. The depressed individual fills out the questionnaires, while one or more of the other family members meet with the therapist. This procedure will continue until the therapist has collected the necessary information from the appropriate subsystems.

In accordance with clinical research strategy, both interview and self-report measures should be used to assess both depressive symptomatology and changes in response to treatment. Systems for measuring depression in adults is (SADS), the Schedule for Affective Disorders and Schizophrenia was developed by Endicott and Spitzer (1978). The SADS covers not only depression, but also such diagnostic categories as schizophrenia, anxiety disorders, and personality disorders. The Hamilton Rating Scale for Depression (HRSD) is also used (1960) and remains the most frequently used interviewer-rated measure of depression. The Child Assessment Schedule (CAS Hodges, Kline, Stern, Cytryn, & McKnew, 1982) is a structured psychological interview for clinical assessment of children between the ages of 7 and 12 years. Self-Report measuring methods are also used in assessing depressive symptomatology.

There are a number of areas of the patient's history and current functioning about which the therapist should inquire. With respect to historical information, the therapist should determine the patient's family history of depression, that is, is there a history of depression in the patient's first-degree relatives? The therapist should also inquire about the patient's personal history of depression. Is this the first episode the patient has experienced, or have there been previous episodes? This area of inquiry will be particularly important in making a decision in the use of antidepressant medication. Any significant medical history should be explored to determine the primary or secondary nature of the current depressive episode. It is also imperative that the therapist determine the patient's potential for suicidal behavior, and consequently, if the patient does not do so, the therapist must introduce the subject of suicide into the interview. If the therapist has reason to believe that the patient presents a risk of suicide, appropriate action must be taken. Hospitalization is one possibility, but this should be considered only in severe cases. Alcohol and drug use should also be assessed historically.

A great amount of information is not yet known about the mapping of different marital and family systems to therapeutic strategies. Nevertheless, the assessment instruments offer the therapist a relatively quick and comprehensive overview of the couple or the family's relationships, information that might take far longer to elicit through interviews only.

Through the administration of these various measures, the therapist should be able to test hypotheses generated throughout the initial part of the assessment interview. The nature and the purpose of the data derived from the questionnaires that are completed by the family members may initially generate an overwhelming amount of information. However, these initial feelings of inundation dissipate rapidly with repeated use of the measures. There are many advantages to the therapist of utilizing standardized assessment instruments instead of, or in addition to, relying only on hunches or intuition.[37]

Chapter X
Counseling/Treatment of Depression

Because of the relative immaturity of marital and family therapy, and in particular, systems treatment for depression, it is difficult to turn to the therapy outcome literature for guidelines in deciding when to and when not to use interpersonal systems therapy. For some therapists, this issue simply does not arise, these therapists maintain that marital/family therapy is the treatment of choice in all cases in which psychotherapy is indicated.

System therapy may be indicated when systems are viewed by the clinician to be embedded in dysfunctional family relationships, or are conceptualized as an expression of the family's pain. Systems therapy is also commonly suggested as the treatment of choice when a child or adolescent is the presenting patient, and when the couple or family itself perceives the difficulties as caused by, or affecting their relationships with one another. Systems therapy also should be considered if depression in one family member seems to be related to recent systematic improvement in another member or, more generally, to the behavior of another family member.

With respect to contradictions for system-oriented therapy, there may be practical limitations, such as the unavailability of key family members, which will prevent the formation of an effective therapeutic relationship. One or more family members may also indicate a strong preference to work with the therapist on an individual basis, and it is unlikely that systems therapy implemented, under duress, would be effective.

The introduction stage begins with the first telephone contact requesting an appointment. The therapist's first task is to gather sufficient information to determine who in the family needs to come for the first session. The therapist can offer a number of responses that might help the person coming in to see the value and importance of having other family members involved in the treatment, if and when it is necessary.

The social stage is important to the system to insure that all family members feel comfortable as possible and to leave everyone with the impression that they will all be involved in the therapy process and have an important contribution to make. The therapist must realize that most families enter therapy feeling defensive end embarrassed, and attempts to ease these feelings must be initiated immediately. Any attempts by family members to launch right into the problem must be blocked by the therapist until everyone has been made to feel reasonably comfortable. The therapist begins the observational and assessment process on greeting the family.

The problem identification stage allows the therapist to elicit from each family member what they see as the problem and why each feels they are at the session.

During the entire exploration phase the therapist is observing everyone's behavior and reactions. It is particularly important, when one person is talking, for the therapist to observe the reactions of the other family members.

Entry into the interaction stage should be a gradual and natural extension of the previous stage. The therapist will slowly draw back from being the center of the discussion, as family members are encouraged to speak to each other directly regarding the opinions expressed previously.

The final activity to be accomplished in this session is to set the ground rules for therapy. The therapist and family may set a time frame in number of sessions to work with. A review may be at the end of the sessions aimed at evaluating the progress made, examining the treatment goals, and making any necessary revisions. The need for further sessions can also be assessed at this time. Family sessions run 1 1/2 hours long, whereas individual sessions and meetings with couples should run approximately 1 hour. With the agreed upon sessions, the therapist and the family can now begin the therapy.

In the action stage, the therapist must utilize all the collected information to promote healthier functioning and produce the desired changes.

The therapist will evaluate all things to provide the support needed for his hypothesis that the patient's depression stemmed largely from her inability to elicit the kind of behavior she wished from her husband. The couple was trapped in a pattern of interactions that prevented either of them from having their needs met.

As this session draws to a close, the therapist uses the technique of reframing, and reframes this interactional sequence in a positive way, with the purpose of providing the family with an alternative perspective for viewing the patient's problematic behavior.

A follow-up session should be scheduled to assess the stability of the gains made at the end of therapy. Again, all relevant psychological inventories should be re-administered, the original treatment goals and gains are reviewed, and the family's current level of functioning is discussed. If necessary, a limited number of treatment sessions with specific goals can be negotiated.[38]

Conclusion

Can depression be prevented? The answer is, probably "no, not completely". We all experience disappointments, losses, rejections and failures which lead to periods of discouragement and unhappiness. For some people, those periods are rare and brief. For others, the depression is more prevalent and long-lasting. It may not be possible or even desirable to prevent times of discouragement, but long-lasting depressions are preventable. There are a number of ways in which this can be done.

Writing from prison, the Apostle Paul once stated that he learned to be content in all circumstances. Knowing that God gives us strength and can supply all our needs, Paul had learned how to live joyfully, both in poverty and in prosperity. Through his experiences, and undoubtedly through a study of the Scriptures, Paul had learned to trust in God and this helped to prevent depression. As in the time of Paul, a conviction that God is alive and in control can give hope and encouragement today, even when we are inclined to be discouraged and without hope. If we can teach this lesson as Christian counselors, that discouragements need not hit as hard as they might otherwise hit.[39]

The second verse of a famous hymn proclaims that "we should never be discouraged" if we take things to the Lord in prayer. This is a popular view for which there is no Scriptural support. Jesus warned that we would have problems and the Apostle James wrote that trials and temptations would come to test our faith and teach us patience. It is unrealistic to smile and laugh in such circumstances, pretending that we're never going to be discouraged. When we are realistic enough to expect pain and informed enough to know that God is always in control, then we can handle discouragement better and often keep from slipping into a deep depression.

Children and adults can be overprotected. This interferes with their ability to learn how to cope or to master the stress of life. If people can see how others cope, and learn how to cope themselves, then circumstances seem less overwhelming and depression is less likely. A concerned group of people who have learned to be caring can do much to soften the trauma of crises and provide strength and help in times of need. Aware that they are not alone, people in crisis are able to cope better and thus avoid severe depression.

Introduction to Marriage and Family Counseling

As we start the subject of marriage and family counseling/therapy, it is well to consider preventive counseling. There are numerous reasons for the present instability and breakdown in and of the marriage. Undoubtedly, one source of the problem concerns the lack of care with which many marriages are put together. Built primarily on sexual attraction, the desire to escape from a difficult home situation, a vague feeling of love, or some equally fleeting motive, many marriage relationships are too flimsy to survive the pressures, challenges and storms of daily living. Unprepared for the stresses of marriage or for the effort and determination required to make marriage work, many give up and bail out before marriage has been given a chance. That which could be meaningful and fulfilling thus becomes frustrating and personally devastating.

In our society we tend to spend a lot more time getting ready for a wedding than preparing for marriage. As a result many beautiful weddings are followed by a lifetime of misery or, at best, minimal happiness. Even when the marriage starts to break down, it is the unusual, rather than the norm to seek out help. Often, not until the situation with the spouse and other members of the family hits its lowest, will professional help be considered. If some way we could encourage pre-marriage Christian counseling, a preventive counseling approach, many of the "marriage problems" could be eliminated. If we could start with understanding the simple truth of Ephesians 5:22-24, "Wives, submit to your own husband..." and Ephesians 5:25-32, "Husbands, love your wives as Christ loves the church..."[40]

Chapter XI
Developing the Client Relationship

Clinicians differ on the issues of involvement at the point of the initial phone call. It would seem, this is an opportunity to become involved. The number of family members present at the initial session has definite implications regarding who will be present at future sessions. There is a far greater likelihood of ongoing commitments to therapy coming from those present in the first session than from those not present initially. For this reason, among others, the family therapist is well advised to take intake calls rather than having a secretary do so. This places the therapist in a better position to initiate the battle for structure. This is called essential by Napier & Whitaker, (1978). At this point of intake, the therapist can communicate who should attend the first session and begin to establish the tone and structure of the therapy.

Once the family is present for the first session, ask the person who called to review what was discussed during the intake call. This serves to communicate that it is important for all to have the benefit of shared understanding, and, hopefully, it eliminates any concerns those not present during the call my have about that initial conversation. Couples and families seen in clinical practice are frequently fragmented in many ways. They present considerable disagreement over problem areas and differences in the intensity of their feelings about them. The clinician who does not make an extensive effort to clarify the presenting problems is doomed to operating in a disoriented and fragmented fashion as the dysfunctional family.

The act of delineating the problems of a dysfunctional and chaotic family can often be the first therapeutic intervention. Simply clarifying the family member's issues can prove helpful as they begin to understand what has been contributing to the chaos they experience. Frequently it is helpful to label the various identified problems as clutter that prevents the clients from securing the kind of family/marital life they hope for. Once the clutter is identified, you can determine where to initially direct efforts to eliminate it from the family operation. The process of clarifying the problem also provides the couple/family with a sense of the clinician's competence and capacity for appropriately managing their destructive process. Although the client's perception that care emanates from the therapist has been extensively acknowledged to be important, the test of competence seems just as important, if not more so, in work with families. In fact, if this sense of competence is not perceived by clients, why should they extend the effort and money necessary to keep future appointments? Each person present should be given the opportunity to express what they perceive to be the problem, and what they feel needs to be changed.

Another point to consider regarding clarification of the problem is, why consider them at this time? In most cases the problems presented are not acute in nature, but have been present for some considerable period of time. Determining what brings the family members in at this time can provide valuable information to the clinician about their attempts to resolve the problems on their own. A good sense of just how creative the group members are will become evident. Also, the counselor will learn what approach not to attempt because the family implemented a solution and it failed. The next point of consideration involves determining and changing the family's perceptual context of the problem. To assess this area, think along the lines of a "bad-sad" continuum. If a family member identifies another member's problem in terms that might be called "bad" – angry, mean, vindictive – framing the problem as possibly being stimulated by "sad" factors – hurt, depressed, lonely, isolated – can be beneficial.

Certainly great sensitivity must be exercised in this area so that a person with a heavy investment in perceiving a problem in a particular way does not end up feeling abused by the therapist.

The genogram is a tool that has been around for some time. Its symbol and mapping tools were popularized by Murray Bowen, and the genogram procedure is endorsed and described in nearly every family therapy text. Consequently, many clinicians use the genogram in the initial stage of therapy to assess family history and as a way to get acquainted.

In some styles of therapy, a great amount of detail is gathered during the genogram. Dates of marriages, deaths, divorces, births, and ages of family members across as many generations as possible are dutifully written down. For the genogram commonly used in the initial phase of therapy, however, less is more, might be the guiding dictum. The most useful information produced by the genogram is not the family structure, but the nature of the relationships making up the structure.

The therapist must direct the spouses to consider the influences from their families of origin that affect the style of their marriage.

There are several additional points to keep in mind while conducting a genogram. Because it is often an initial task of therapy, the clinician needs to maintain the involvement of all the family members throughout the experience. Typically, one branch of the family tree is dealt with at a time. All members of the family need to be kept as involved as can be, as everyone is asked to participate.

Teaching clients about themselves, their family, and about families in general has the equally important goal of maintaining a balance of social exchange during the initial phase of therapy. The therapy relationship, like other interpersonal relationships, proceeds through several phases.

Some therapists place great emphasis on discovering the expectations each partner had about a marital partner prior to marriage. The courtship phase of the relationship is best discussed by referring to major events such as first intercourse, first item purchased together, major fights and the like, that both spouses can remember. In like manor, the history of the marriage can be discussed.

Most clients enter family therapy without a clear idea of what will happen or what they will do. It becomes the counselor's responsibility to help the family understand what to expect.

Through all phases of therapy, many new concepts may be presented to the family. In the initial phase of therapy, the concept of family system is often defined to help clients differentiate between family therapy and individual therapy. In the middle phase, the same concept can be used as the rational for a reframing of presenting systems and other family problems. In the terminal phase of therapy, the concept is helpful in clarifying what changes in family organization may be necessary to accommodate upcoming developmental crisis in family life.

Establishing goals is every bit as important for the therapist as it is for the family. For the therapist, goal establishment helps achieve feedback about the impact of interventions. Such feedback can be significant in preventing the burnout that stems from a sense of aimlessness. Without some specific direction and focus, it is easy for a therapist to question effectiveness, especially if a family or couple questions the value of therapy.

Recognizing that families are composed of individuals, it is important to acknowledge that family readiness for change, in varying degrees, lies within each member. Consequently, the clinician needs to assess the levels of readiness or motivation of each member in order to avoid making therapeutic moves that would alienate those least motivated. Along with each member's level of readiness, the clinician needs to be alert to the individual's power or potency with the family organization. The clinician who is unaware of the individual's level of readiness and power could easily end up not only being unsuccessful in drawing families into therapy, but may actually push them out.

One of the goals of the assessment process is to determine the health of the family system. The process demands that the therapist make value judgments in which the client family, its structure, and intersection progresses are compared to a model family or against some standard familiar to the therapist.

Rules are part of every relationship, and family rules are the dynamic components of the family's organization. The obvious rules govern who takes out the garbage, who mows the lawn, who does which housecleaning task, and the like, but numerous rules of a more subtle nature exist. They are the internalized implicit regulations that maintain a family's systemic functioning, valuable to know in developing a therapeutic plan.

The family myth is part of the pervasive ideology of the family that evolves from the interaction of the family's rituals, roles, and rules. The therapist should comprehend this ideology, or the family's definition of framing of reality, before developing interventions.

Disengagement is an important concept in differentiating among families as to the family's level of intimacy and the strength of family members' personal identities. As with all system analysis, knowledge of the purpose served by a given level of disengagement is internal to effective treatment.

Parent identification is a concept frequently used in the assessment of families. It is most often applied to a child who has taken on the role of parent or spouse in his or her family, although it could just as easily be used to describe any family member in another role who assumes an adult role in a family of procreation. The term is easy to misuse, because, in healthy family systems, we expect to see children try out roles. In assessing parent identification, the clinician pays attention to the frequency, duration, system context, and impact on child development of inappropriate role taking.

Even though sexuality plays an important role in marital life, family therapists have tended to believe that sexual problems result from relationship dysfunction and to refer clients with such problems to sex therapists.

Alcohol and drugs have come to be recognized as a major problem within families. A 1983 Gallup poll indicated that one-third of all respondents reported that at least one person in their family had what they regarded as a significant drug problem. Because of the pervasive nature of this problem, it is important for the clinician to know how to identify a problem, and what to do once it is recognized.

Although most marriage and family therapists do not receive many referrals to resolve specific work problems, work-related behaviors certainly influence family dynamics and vice versa.

In the last twenty-five years, extensive research and attention has been given to the hypothesis that the stress of life's accumulated events is an important factor in the etiology of somatic and psychiatric disorders. As the body attempts to maintain a state of homeostasis or equilibrium, any life event that upsets that steady state demands adaptation. Similarly, families whose steady states are upset by life events must adapt.

Just as it is valuable to routinely assess the presence of stressors in a family, it is always appropriate to explore the presence of stressors or changes that preceded the development of a specific problem presented in therapy. This assessment is important to determine whether the problem is evidence of worsened by a faulty adaptation to a particular stressor.

Sexual and physical abuses are frequently found to coexist in families. Their long term destructive effects are obvious. Although relationship problems sometimes promote and maintain these problems, these behaviors themselves often confound and entrench family difficulties. Therefore, astute therapists should be sensitive to detecting abuse in order to ensure that they provide appropriate treatment.

To determine if sexual/physical abuse is present in the family, therapists need to be comfortable enough with their own values and attitudes to approach families in a matter-of-fact, but sensitive, fashion. Calm and direct questioning of the family can provide an atmosphere of permission absent from the family before therapy. Such an approach communicates to the family members that the therapist is not intimidated by abuse problems, and it also establishes a counter-rule to the no-talk rule frequently observed in these families. The therapist needs to convey a sense of competence and strength, while simultaneously establishing the important counter-rule.

Clinicians are currently encountering parents with sexually abused children far more frequently than what has been the case in even the recent past. As a society appears to have broken the taboo that inhibited people from disclosing this experience and enhanced methods of identification have developed, the incidence of reporting has increased.

As the public develops a greater awareness of the problem known as codependency, helpers can expect to hear more as a self-diagnosis. When working with families that diagnose themselves in this way, you must proceed with caution and not be too quick to assume that your understanding of codependency is the same as theirs.

The technique of circular questioning, used as an assessment tool, has the unique value of placing clients in a meta-position, outside of the system they are currently embroiled in. As the family members listen to another member respond to circular questioning, they also may learn for the first time other members' perception of the family operation. Circular questioning also tends to elicit information in a nonthreatening way and especially can help clients who have difficulty expressing themselves directly. Circular questioning can be a powerful tool to employ during the assessment phase of therapy and at other times, also. Besides generating valuable information for the therapist, it can also begin to expose the family to itself in new ways that promote new understanding. Further, it can speed the gathering of information, overcoming the problems of various family members' feeling too shy to talk and of family rules that do not allow family members to directly share the information another member offers about them in response to the circular questioning.[41]

Chapter XII
Teaching

Teaching is a most important therapist skill that is not talked about by authors of family therapy texts or by supervisors. Teaching, in the context of therapy, is an individualized process that consists of showing clients how to do something that will improve family functioning or relating information that will change client attitudes in order to motivate family members into action. The important elements of successful teaching in therapy are (1) a well-defined ability to know when to switch into a teaching mode, (2) awareness of what it is that the clients need to be taught and what they can learn in the context of a single therapy session or part of a session, (3) the ability to demonstrate what the clients are to learn and to clearly present new ideas when attitude change is in order, and (4) well-developed skills in providing actual instruction.

The key to success in teaching is to use a systematic training procedure, following three basic steps. First, a rationale for learning the skill is presented to the clients. Second, the skill is demonstrated. Third, the clients practice and receive feedback while they perform the skill.

Typically, the clients will want to discuss the rationale, especially for complex skills. Such discussions are important because misconceptions can be clarified when they occur rather than at some later time when they may result in client failure. In addition, during the discussions, the therapist can usually model using the skill while the discussion occurs and enhance the validity of the rationale in the process. Once clients understand why the skill is important and what the payoffs will be, the skill needs to be demonstrated.

The last stage of the teaching procedure is to have clients practice the skill and receive feedback on their performance. It is at this point in teaching that therapists most often make a mistake. Usually, the mistake is to demonstrate a skill and then to ask the family or couple to continue the discussion that preceded the switch from therapy to teaching, while one family member attempts to practice. Not surprising most clients have difficulty performing the skill well, because the situation used for practice is emotionally charged. Always have clients first practice a skill in a low threat situation. Another important task in this phase is to let clients know that they are performing well, or at least in close approximation to what has been demonstrated.

Once the therapist knows this three-step strategy of teaching, the steps can be applied to many different skills that clients need to help them interact better and feel successful in therapy.

One very important teaching skill is to know when to leave the therapy mode and to enter the teaching mode.

Many of the problems presented by families in therapy involve the skill of the parental subsystem in carrying out the parenting role. As a result, the therapist is often called upon to show the adults how to parent. Unfortunately, many therapists do not have a detailed knowledge of basic parenting skills, and all too often, therapists' recommendations are not understood, or they are forgotten, because time is not taken to teach clients how to carry them out. This is a very important teaching requirement in the therapy process.

In teaching the method of child control, the mistake most often made by therapists is in not requiring the parents to role-play placing the child in time-out during a therapy session. Instead, many therapists merely describe how to institute the procedure and then check up on its success the following week. For effective learning, the parent must be supervised while sending a child to time-out.[42]

Chapter XIII
Therapy Process Procedures

Once the initial phase of therapy has been completed, it is time to undertake the middle phase in which most of the work takes place.

Small talk is an important part of all therapy, but especially of family therapy. Upon first meeting, individuals use chitchat as a way to get acquainted. After we come to know another person, we use chitchat as a preface to further interaction. Within a group of people, such as a client group, however, small talk is more likely to dominate verbal interaction unless the group is moved toward its tasks. Small talk can inhibit the progress of therapy unless it is controlled. Controlling small talk means initiating it at the beginning of a session and then quickly communicating that the session is beginning through a transitional or directive statement.

After the session has started the therapist may find clients who talk on and on, seemingly ignorant of any rules of human interaction. Often, they can pose a real barrier to progress in therapy. Whether the family conspires to encourage the rambling or whether such behavior is engaged in out of habit or due to anxiety, it is the therapist's task to intervene. Most often, a comment that communicates the therapist's feelings of impatience or irritation will change the client's behavior, at least for one session. When other family members are also frustrated by parent or sibling rambling, they can be encouraged to express their own needs to talk and their feelings of not being able to do so. The situation in which nothing is effective is the most trying and leads therapists to have thoughts of letting the person talk until spent and to consider paradoxical strategies of encouraging more rambling. However, a different approach deserves mention because it works well.

First, note that the chief difficulty of interacting with nonstop ramblers is how to gain the floor without awkwardly grabbing it. Most people are socialized not to interrupt or speak while someone else is speaking. We hesitate to barge in on someone's discourse in order to avoid feeling guilty and insensitive. As therapists, we fear that we may model an awkward interruption for our clients. As a result of not knowing how to interrupt and gain the floor, we permit our clients to continue unchecked. However, a way to intercept without awkwardness and take the floor is available.

The procedure consists of two steps which are based on the idea that even the most stubborn of ramblers will stop to listen to a simple reflection or summary of their comments. Consequently, the first step consists of verbally or nonverbally capturing the client's attention and then summarizing the client's thoughts and feelings. Then, before the client has a chance to reply or continue talking, the therapist takes command of the floor by asking questions directed toward another family member or by directing the verbal interaction toward some other topic; this will allow the therapist to maintain control of the floor.

Right from the start of therapy, it is most effective to institute the rule that people are to speak for no one but themselves. In the initial interview, for example, parents may try to speak for children or one spouse for another. If after several interruptions, the family does not comply with this rule, the therapist must address the problem directly, in such a way that it cannot be misunderstood. Refusing to accommodate a family's usual communication pattern is a powerful, destabilizing tactic. It may take several sessions for those who have been silent to open up.

There are several ways to encourage clients to speak directly to one another without expressly telling them to do so. The first way is to phrase a request specifying who is to be spoken to. If this approach does not work, the therapist can explain that in family therapy the partners should feel free to interact with one another, and that frequently they will be directed to do so.

At times, clients will want to take potshots at one another. These verbal potshots are most often short, quick-delivered, hit-and-run statements designed to gain some momentary interpersonal advantage. Name calling, using words such as never and always in an accusation, and assigning motive are examples of potshots. If the therapist does not take steps to prevent such behavior and does not intervene when potshots first appear, then clients may rightly assume that they are to behave in sessions just as they do at home. If therapy is to be successful, however, clients must learn to behave differently.

Throughout therapy, one important task that belongs to the therapist is to help clients communicate with one another more clearly and avoid the traps created by undefined labels. As in any relationship, the therapeutic relationship develops along with the acceptance of certain concepts and labels used to describe important feeling states. Unless these labels are mutually understood by all participants in therapy, the prospect of change may be limited because the lexicon of communication symbols is not shared.

One important aspect of any form of therapy is the management of client attention. Clients suffering from depression, for instance, focus attention on their feelings and thoughts of gloom, whereas clients with paranoid ideation focus attention on behavior and inventions of others to confirm their suspicions of betrayal or harm. Similarly, family members tend to blame an identified patient for family problems and focus their attention on the person in an attempt to confirm their beliefs. Managing client attention requires that the therapist not only maintain an awareness of what clients are attending to from not only second to second, but also structure sessions so that clients can easily follow the topics of discussion. The therapist must provide an adequate transition between topics.

Unsolved grief sometimes serves as an emotional brake to the development of a family. The family that does not successfully mourn losses often stops growing. Losses may come in the form of physical death, loss of an ideal, divorce or other loss of a significant relationship, not receiving an important promotion, not completing an academic goal such as graduation, or a child marrying someone other than the parents had desired. Therapists need to remember that losses comprise many human experiences besides the obvious one, death. There may be times in working with a family when a crisis should be induced. At times when the client's anxiety levels have fallen too low, and the uneasiness or tension that can be so important to stimulating change is lost. At these times the therapist might consider inducing a crisis by amplifying a particular deviation already present or manipulating the family's affect so that dynamic tension is rekindled.

Just as there are times when therapy can benefit from the therapist's inducing a crisis, at other times, productive therapy dictates that a crisis be defused. To diffuse a crisis, therapists have the option of using themselves to create an intentional triangle or referring the family to its past crisis to activate resources that helped them in earlier circumstances.

Confrontation is a valuable though potentially explosive, technique when used appropriately. Just as nuclear power has tremendous positive value to mankind, yet equally distractive power, confrontation has the same potential in relationship to family therapy. In general, confrontation has its greatest therapeutic value after the development of a relationship that provides for adequate shock-absorbing quality. If confrontation is engaged in without evident caring and commitment, it can be perceived as caustic or designed solely to injure. Certainly, confrontation is a procedure that could provoke termination by the family, but, perhaps more importantly, create an impression for the family that all therapy is more injurious than it is helpful so that they never seek help.

As defined by the lay person, confrontation is a hostile, unpleasant, demanding, and anxiety provoking experience that is best avoided. These feelings result from confrontations in relationships and encounters that produce frustration, irritation, and anger.

On occasions a member of the client unit may abruptly leave the session amidst an intense display of emotion. In view of the intensity of affect often observed among family members, the therapist should not be surprised by this occurrence. It often provides important new observational data about family organization and operation.

Reframing, as the procedure is called in the context of therapy, is designed to change the client's view of their problems. Family therapists especially recognize that client's definitions of their problems often perpetuate those problems by narrowing the range of possible solutions. Consequently, a first step in changing how clients act often consists of attempting to reframe systems and problems so new solutions can be tried out. Reframing is most successful when the therapist attempts to actively persuade family members that the reframe is not only a plausible reconceptualization of their problems, but also more accurate than their old conception. Therapists correctly assume that they are psychologically important to their clients, and that their approval can help clients change. The ways of showing that approval range from making a long statement that might follow successful completion of homework to simply stating "Good". The longer statement has the most effect if it is stated in terms of the therapist's feelings. Shorter rewarding remarks typically are used in situations when skills are being taught in session. When a spouse responds appropriately during a session in which a couple is being taught problem solving, for instance, a quick, unobtrusively stated "good" immediately after an effective response will communicate approval. In teaching situations, such remarks need to occur frequently until the client knows what is expected. Appropriate behavior, if it is to continue and generalize, requires attention supplied through social reinforcement.

Frequently, in the midst of a session, a therapist will observe an interaction between clients that plays a role in maintaining either the symptom or a dysfunctional family structure. The dilemma is whether to interrupt the session and change the interaction or let it go, hoping it will occur again at a more opportune time. Experience will be the best guide on whether to intervene. Generally, however, it is best to intervene rather than wait until later; a better opportunity may not present itself.

The opportunity to observe how parents interact with their children can prove invaluable to the therapist. As with most interactional behavior, though, eventually patterns already observed repeat themselves, a little, if any, new behavior is observed. It is very valuable for the therapist to promote and observe any new behaviors among parents with disruptive children. One procedure to implement with disruptive children is to encourage the parents to intervene with them. This gives the therapist the chance to observe parenting styles and offer feedback on how the parents might improve or add to the management styles and repertoire.

Few parents can avoid developing feelings of fondness for those who positively attend to their young children. Consequently, therapists who are kind, attentive, and interactive with a family's young children are bound to engender fondness in the parents toward them. To avoid this simple, but powerful means of initially joining the family is a gross oversight; such attention can serve to model, for one or both parents, how to effectively interact with young children. Typically it will be more valuable for the father than for the mother.

At times the therapist will have only one partner show up for the session. When this happens a choice is presented to the therapist, whether to go ahead with the session with one partner, or wait until the next time both can attend. Generally speaking, if a therapeutic alliance is established with the couple, an individual session can occur without damage, assuming certain precautions are taken. On the other hand, if it is doubtful that the alliance has been established with the couple, an individual session could prove difficult to the development of future couple-oriented work.

The laws of child abuse, physical and sexual, must be taken into consideration. The twenty-four hour reporting law, as well as dealing with suicide threats are at the forefront of possibilities at all times. Recognizing the systems of alcohol and drug abuse is highly regarded by experienced therapists as a necessity when working in family therapy.

Clinicians who are not prepared for regression at some point are at risk to perceive a slip as a personal affront to their professional competence. If perceived in this fashion, the therapist may be quick to become judgmental and make a bad situation worse. At this time, and in this way, the clinician is no longer a catalyst for change but rather another problem for the family. The therapist must guard against this.[43]

Chapter XIV
Case Management

To manage families through the process of therapy effectively and to supply services in a professional manner, therapists need to know how to call on outside sources, how to get paid, how to keep notes, and how to perform a host of other case management aspects of family therapy.

Sometimes it may seem difficult even to take a vacation. Everyone needs a break in the routine of daily work, and family therapists are no different. The problem may be how to create the needed space in the appointment calendar without feeling irresponsible.

Clients can cope quite well, even if their therapist is on an extended vacation, if they are notified well in advance and if they know what to do in case of a crisis. An upcoming vacation should be first mentioned approximately four sessions beforehand and again at each session until the vacation begins. Vacations can be taken quite easily with this approach.

When a referral needs to be made it can present a problem in family therapy, and can be one of the most insidious and potentially compromising to the success of treatment. Nevertheless, the importance of the referring person to therapy needs to be considered. Frequently, the referring person may have become intimately involved in the family's organization and operation and, without realizing it, could prove to be a significant homeostatic force in family therapy. It is important that the family therapist ascertain the role and function of the referring person in the family's life. Often, this can be expedited by inviting the referring person to the first session. During this session, prior involvements and a history can be secured, and more importantly, future roles, expectations, and means of communicating can be established and agreed upon. Some of the reasons for referring may be, but not limited to the following; 1) the therapist or family is relocating; 2) the clients present a unique problem requiring that a different orientation or specialty become clinically involved; or 3) the therapist and/or family determine they are unable to negotiate a viable therapeutic contract.

There are also occasions when the therapist may choose to be joined by a co-therapist. This may be done for a multitude of reasons, such as becoming "stuck" with a family and wanting new input, facilitating the training/supervisory process of a therapist, or choosing as a matter of personal preference to function with a co-therapist when none has been previously available.

There may be times when the practicing family therapist will introduce a consultant to the therapeutic system. Examples are when 1) a family presents concern for a child's learning problems and a psychologist may be introduced to do an assessment, or 2) the family therapist may feel stuck and want to introduce a consultant for one or two sessions to provide new insight and impetus to the therapy. Naturally, these two reasons may also be combined, as when a family presents itself with a member who is concerned about having been sexually abused as a child, possibly drug dependent, or has some other problem that would prompt the family therapist to introduce a consultant.

Discussing fee for service should not be set aside for any reason. Fees for service are a fact of life and should be dealt with up front, directly by the family therapist. This allows the therapist a potentially valuable therapeutic opportunity. If the couple/family has insurance that will pay for the service, the receptionist can likely handle the necessary paperwork, but there is much value in the therapist's handling those situations in which the clients pay directly for the service.

The issue of termination in family therapy is not nearly so crucial an issue as it is portrayed to be when working from an individual perspective. Family therapy is oriented to facilitating family members' coming to use one another, rather than the therapy, as primary resources. The notion of cure is not nearly as prominent in family therapy as it is with individuals, because families are continually evolving through a life cycle with predictably difficult times and because of family therapy's tendency to be more problem specific than is most individual therapy.

One way of reducing, if not eliminating, the issue of termination is to work on the basis of specific temporal boundaries. From the onset of therapy, there is agreement among all involved that therapy will last for a certain number of sessions. If the agreement is to meet for five sessions, it is understood that everyone, including the therapist, will decide if they have accomplished the goals by the fifth session and then enter into a decision making process about the value/need of negotiating for more sessions to reach a particular goal. If an agreement to continue is reached, the purpose and time frame is once again agreed upon. As a result, everyone grains a temporal orientation similar to those to which we have grown accustomed in daily life. At the end of each negotiated time period, the therapist can facilitate the discussion about continuing with another block of time for treatment, and/or encourage clients to go home and discuss continuing and then contact the therapist with the decision.

The therapist should take, in a large part, the ownership of the marriage and family therapy as a profession. Know that procedures exist in the practice of marriage and family therapy. Reject the notion that family therapy is a mere group of connected ideas easily adapted to any sort of mental health practice. There is a way to go about the effective practice of family therapy. The procedures stated need systematic evaluation beyond that conducted by ourselves. Nonetheless, if learned and implemented, these procedures represent a good starting point for beginning clinicians and a springboard to developing new procedures for the experienced practitioner.[44]

Chapter XV
The Family and the Bible

Five characteristics of a healthy family:
1. **Love;** Parents express genuine love and affection for each other and their children.
2. **Discipline;** Discipline is considered essential; it is fair, quick, and to the point.
3. **Consistency;** Parents are united on all rules and consistently enforce them.
4. **Example;** Parents live up to the standards that they expect their children to observe.
5. **Authority;** Parental authority is established and respected and the husband has the final authority in the home.

Let's look at the above areas closer and consider them in light of what God has to say through His Word, the Bible.

What is love? Love is much more than an emotion, though it has a large emotional component. Love affects an individual's entire being. God has designed human beings to share love on three planes, spiritual, emotional, and physical. The complete absence of love (rejection) can destroy a person emotionally and in some cases physically.

Ideally, love should be as the apostle Paul stated in 1 Corinthians 13.[45] That type of love, termed agape in Greek, does not seek anything in return, not even acceptance of itself, its first concern is for the other person. It is a self-sacrificing love. Agape in its absolute form denotes God's love, not human love. Christians regard Christ's crucifixion as the supreme manifestation of God's love, since Christ died for helpless, sinful, unworthy human beings (Romans 5:5-8).[46]

In contrast to agape, is the Greek word eros. Eros is self-centered love, wanting something in return for what it gives. Seeking self-gratification, erotic love tends to exploit and take advantage of someone for personal ends. It is also known as conditional love.

A third type of love is denoted by the Greek word phileo. Phileo is passed in an inner communication and mutual attraction between the person loving and the person loved. That kind of friendship feeling is commonly called brotherly love. Healthy or genuine love is essential for a good home environment.

Modern day professionals aren't the only ones concerned about genuineness of parental love for children. According to the Bible, God showed a greater concern nearly three thousand years ago, with the words, "He who spares the rod hates his son, but he who loves him is careful to discipline him" (Proverbs 13:24).[47] One way to show genuine love for our children is to discipline them (in love) when they need it. Positive reinforcement is another way of showing genuine love for a child. It is extremely important that each child be considered a significant person. Each child, no matter how young, needs to feel important.

The love of God is a vital foundation for a healthy family. The Bible commands us to love God with all our hearts, soul, and might (Deuteronomy 6:5).[48] Loving God is good preparation for loving others. Jesus said, "A new commandment I give to you. Love one another. As I have loved you, so you must love one another. All men will know you are my disciples if you love one another". (John 13:34-35)[49] The apostle John wrote, "And this is His command, to believe in the name of His Son, Jesus Christ, and to love one another as He commanded us" (1 John 3:23).[50] God promises to reward men and women for having enough love in their hearts to live by His principles. Jesus said, "Whoever has my commands and obeys them, he is the one who loves me. He who loves me will be loved by my Father, and I too will love him and show myself to him." (John 14:21)[51]

Love between husband and wife must be genuine for a healthy home. Most neurotic mother-child relationships partially result from the mother being unfulfilled in her love needs, both emotional and physical, by her husband. The apostle Paul wrote, "Husbands love your wives, just as Christ loved the Church and gave himself up for her to make her holy, cleansing her by the washing with water through the Word, and to present her to Himself as a radiant Church, without stain or wrinkle or any other blemish, but holy and blameless. In this same way, husbands ought to love their wives as their own bodies. He who loves his wife loves himself. After all, no one ever hated his own body, but he feeds and cares for it, just as Christ does the Church, for we are members of His Body. (Ephesians 5:25-30)[52] Note that "He who loves his wife loves himself" (v. 28b). Loving oneself in a healthy manner is essential for developing intimate love with a mate.

Discipline is a word most don't like to use today. God states this quite plain, "Train up a child in the way that he should go, and when he is old he will not turn from it". (Proverbs 22:6)[53] "Do not withhold discipline from a child, if you punish him with the rod, he will not die. Punish him with the rod and save his soul from death." (Proverbs 23:13-14)[54]

Parental consistency is essential for healthy development of children. To feel secure, children must know their limits. When limits are not predetermined and consistently enforced, confusion arises.

Children learn much of their behavior from their parents. They do what their parents do more often than what their parents say they should do.

Good example should be extended beyond family into the community. God warns that any "overseer" in a church (pastor, deacon, elder) "must manage his own family well and see that his children obey him with proper respect. If anyone does not know how to manage his own family, how can he take care of God's Church?" (1 Timothy 3:4-

5)[55] Fathers who fail to manage their own family well do not set a good example and hence, should consider their families condition.[56]

Conclusion

For various reasons today, an increasing number of children are growing up in one-parent families. Through the grace of God it is possible for a widowed mother, or a young father whose wife has deserted him and their children, to go it alone in child-raising. The poignant difficulties experienced in such situations, however, demonstrate that families are healthiest when a father and mother cooperate in the task of parenting. Struggle for leadership between father and mother can produce neurotic children, as can the absence of a parent. The father's role in the family is extremely important, though often neglected. Many men, their energies exhausted by their role as sole breadwinner, come home from work with little desire to play a leadership role at home. Their wives may feel envious of their supposedly more satisfying role in the world outside the home. Having no other sphere in which to exercise authority, such women sometimes become domineering at home. The vast majority of emotionally disturbed adults grew up in a home governed by a strong smothering mother and a weak father who neglected his parenting leadership responsibilities. A child's life may be determined by his or her identity with the parent of the same sex as well as by the interactions of the parents.

The biblical concept of headship is under much discussion at this present time. It is clear that Jesus Christ should be the ultimate head of every Christian home, as He is of the whole Church. The husband and wife are equal in importance but have different biblical roles when it comes to leadership in the home. Perhaps the majority of Christians interpret Ephesians 5:23 to mean that the man should have his way in all situations where there is disagreement,[57] in spite of the model of humble servant-leadership by Jesus Christ in His own teachings (Mark 10:45)[58] and His own example (Matthew 11:29; Philippians 2:5-8).[59]

If the husband is the president, the wife should be the executive vice-president. In some families, however, the husband, as president, treats his wife like the secretary, filing clerk, and janitress all put together. This is not healthy or biblical. From the beginning God said "It is not good for the man to be alone. I will make a helper suitable for him" (Genesis 2:18).[60] Yet that same Hebrew word for helper, Helpmeet in the KJV, is used most often in the Bible to refer to God himself in His role of helping His people (Exodus 18:4, Deuteronomy 33:7, Psalms 70:5, Hosea 13:9).[61] This does not refer to a master/slave relationship.

God's words to Eve after her sin were "Your desire will be for your husband and he will rule over you" (Genesis 3:16).[62] God intended harmony, not conflict, between the sexes. However, passages such as Colossians 3:18 "Wives, submit to your husbands, as it is fitting in the Lord",[63] which speak of the subjection or submission of women, have long been misused by men to justify prideful dictatorship. God desires for the husband to be the final authority in the home, but husbands should be reminded also that Ephesians 5:21 tells all Christians, and family members in particular, to "Submit to one another out of reverence for Christ."[64]

Much pressure is put on Christian counselors to teach truth, as the world is pressuring women to recognize their basic equality with men, which the Bible long ago emphasized in its statement that God created both male and female human beings in "His own image" (Genesis 1:27). Christian counselors have a responsibility to teach understanding of the partnership of men and women as equals under Christ as head of the Church and head of the family, as a legitimate interpretation of how the Bible intends for God's people to live. God commands husbands to "be considerate as you live with your wives, and treat them with respect as the weaker partner as heirs with you of the gracious gift of life, so that nothing will hinder your prayers" (1 Peter 3:7).[65] Men and women are equal in importance in the eyes of God, even though God gave husbands and wives different leadership responsibilities in the home. Clearly, the biblical pattern that Christian counselors must be mindful of is being challenged today, by Christians as well as non-Christians. The world is, in some cases, challenging not only the traditional husband/wife roles, but the institution of the family, and even marriage itself. Some of their complaints are legitimate and should be evaluated. But as Christians, we must not let the world squeeze us into its mold (Romans 12:1),[66] and as Christian therapists we must work within this frame of knowledge to assist. God's advice to husbands and wives in Scripture will always be the best to follow. The concept of authority is best taught by having a father who is willing to assume the leadership role and a mother who is willing to show respect for his authority. It is also best to have two parents who submit to Christ's authority and to each other, respectfully sharing the leadership role, with the husband serving as a humble, loving leader and his wife co-leading in a submissive but assertive way.

Introduction to General Counseling

According to many secular psychologists, people are born as blank slates. This school of thought originated with St. Thomas Aquinas (1225-1274) and was developed further by John Locke (1632-1704) and capitalized on by Sigmund Freud (1856-1939). The neo-Freudians believe that the environment and developmental stages are what determines man's behavior. Although there are effects from the environment and developmental stages, one would be hard pressed to convince the parents of a newborn baby that their child is born a blank slate and has no unique behavior patterns.

General observance of newborns will shoot holes in this theory. (I am the father of eight children, and fifteen grandchildren.) Some newborns will coo sweetly, sleep long hours and only cry when wet, hungry or sick. There are others who will awaken every couple of hours, scream at the top of their lungs and resist any effort to be quieted. There are newborns who will cuddle and laugh for any adult who holds them, and there are some who are comfortable with no one but their mother or father. This is the observed proof of mental ability and uniqueness. If children were born blank, you could see this when you look into a hospital nursery because the babies would all behave in the same way; yet, as you know, each infant is different.

Many people carry hidden resentment toward God for not designing them the way they would have put themselves together; they think of themselves as being too short, too tall, too big of a nose, etc. We need, at times a theory based on the Bible, God's Word, and to learn to trust in what that Word has to say, and build a Christ like character so that we can experience life abundantly. It is foolish to think that we are wiser than God. In Psalms 139:13-16, David wrote:

"For you created my inmost being; you knit me together in my mother's womb. I praise you because I am fearfully and wonderfully made; your works are wonderful, I know that full well. My frame was not hidden from you when I was made in the secret place. When I was woven together in the depths of the earth, your eyes saw my unformed body. All the days ordained for me were written in your book before one of them came to be."[67]

Techniques in therapy based on the assumption that man has evolved and that man is his own god, therefore, teach that a person has within himself/herself the solutions to his/her problems and can never do more than bring some temporary relief. The counseling problems of the past remain unresolved and are becoming far worse.

Full and complete change of a human being is an act of God. It is imperative for a counselor to understand the uniqueness of man and his standing with God now, as well as his unique place in eternity, with the presupposition that man is a created spiritual being, created by God, with a soul and lives in a body.

Chapter XVI
The Time for a Change

You may or may not be aware that in many seminaries, an accepted therapeutic counseling technique that is taught and most widely used among a cross-section of the clergy is what has become known as "client-centered" therapy.

Carl Rogers, a well-known secular psychologist, believed that the greatest and most positive changes that could take place in a person being counseled were brought about by allowing the counselee to talk. In this type of technique the counselor or the therapist seldom say anything other than re-focus and re-direct what they might say, like, "Uh huh, how do you feel about that?" or "You feel angry, " or "You seem frustrated."

Client-centered therapy, along with many other techniques, including Relational Emotive Therapy and types of psychoanalytic therapy, are based on the assumption that man has evolved and that man is his own god. Therefore, a person has within himself/herself the solution to his/her problems.

We can punch holes in this theory by looking at the statistics of the past thirty years, put together by The Heritage Foundation, and published by Empower America, The Heritage Foundation and Free Congress Foundation. Some of the statistics (called The Index of Leading Cultural Indicators) from this report reflect the general direction in which the culture is heading. Let's look at the marriage and divorce rates in our culture.

The number of divorces in America has increased nearly 200 percent in only thirty years. In actual numbers it looks like this: 393, 000 divorces in 1960, compared with 1,175,000 in 1990. This increase in the number of divorces has led to an increase in the number of children directly affected by divorce. According to Bennett's report less than 60 percent of all children in 1990 were living with their biological, married parents. In addition, the percentage of children living with a divorced parent has increased from 2.1 percent in 1960, to 9.5 percent in 1990. In actual numbers, this calculates as 463,000 children in 1960, to 1,005,000 children in 1990. The percentage of children living with single parents has more than tripled in the last thirty years. Today more than 20 million children live in single parent homes. The numbers are as follows, in 1960 there were 9.1 percent living in single parent homes, in 1991 this had increased to 28.6 percent. Although there is controversy surrounding the number of reported abuse cases, the number of children abused in the United States has increased dramatically in the past twenty years.[68] Some of the reasons may include substance abuse, the additional stress of single parenthood, increased likelihood of having a man living in the home not related to the children, and low income status.

Teen suicide, high school dropouts, unwed and teen pregnancies, abortions, and the high crime rate are all indicators of a need to improve the way we convey our family values.[69]

I believe that it is impossible to take therapies built on the assumption of evolution or humanism and modify them for use in a Christian counseling setting. It is time for a Christian alternative as we move into the next century. The problems are not always caused by sin, as we would think of sin. Many problems are a result of the complicated, fast-paced world in which we live, a world that threatens our emotional stability.

The counseling problems of the past, for the most part, go unresolved and are becoming far worse as we come into the twenty-first century. The need is great for Christians to once more become proactive in the counseling process.

Chapter XVII
Types of Models

Sigmund Freud is considered the father of psychiatry. Freud regarded all religion as the "universal neurosis of mankind". Freud, of course, grew up as a Jew in an area where Jews were despised and persecuted by self-righteous people who called themselves Christians. It is no wonder that he had a disgust for what he saw as "Christianity".

One of the areas of which Sigmund Freud spent time and greatly overemphasized was the "Oedipus Complex". This "complex", states that young children between the ages of three and six grow up thinking that somehow they will grow up but the parent of the opposite sex will stay the same age, and that they will somehow replace the parent of the same sex by marrying the parent of the opposite sex.[70]

Another theory of Sigmund Freud's was that all guilt is false guilt and many psychiatrists agree with the Freudian view. The theory of the conscience is what Sigmund Freud called the superego. According to Freud it is molded by the influences of our environment: What our parents taught was right or wrong, what they practice as being right or wrong (not always the same as what they taught), what our church taught was right or wrong, what church members practiced as being right or wrong, what our friends and teachers thought was right or wrong.[71]

Sigmund Freud's "Id" roughly corresponds to what Christians call the "old nature". Freud's "superego" corresponds roughly to the conscience. The "ego" corresponds to the will.[72]

The oldest recognized systematic approach to explaining and treating psychological problems is classical psychoanalysis. Modern psychoanalytic theory is derived primarily from the work of Sigmund Freud, a Viennese neurologist (1856-1939). The theory places major emphasis on the role of the unconscious and of dynamic forces in mental functioning. Treatment using classical psychoanalysis usually requires a patient to lie on a couch facing away from the therapist while the therapist and patient, using several techniques, attempt to uncover subconscious conflicts. The patient is asked to talk about whatever he or she wishes, including memories and feelings. The therapist then asks the patient for thoughts, fantasies, and feelings associated with the material given (free association). Use is also made of the patient's unconscious disproportionate emotional response to the therapist (transference). For instance, the patient may unconsciously respond to the therapist as a father or mother figure. It is believed that such a response can be used to facilitate understanding of the patient's own unconscious feelings toward father, or mother, or spouse.

The therapist observes and points out the patient's resistance to talk about or "work through" various areas of conflict. Dream material is reported and analyzed to obtain a better grasp of the unconscious. The therapist strongly emphasizes clarification of feelings. As awareness of feelings increases, the defense mechanisms that concealed them are also uncovered. Analytic theory states that as patients "experience" acceptance from the analyst, they accept and "love" themselves more and hence, subconscious conflict diminishes. The analyst and patient normally meet for one hour per day, five days a week. An average period of time for classical psychoanalysis is three to five years, but some patients stay in analysis for much longer than that.[73]

Adlerian or "individual" psychology was developed in 1911 by Alfred Adler, a contemporary of Freud. Alfred Adler agreed that human beings have inherent factors that affect their destiny but concluded such factors as social rather than biological. Rather than being mentally sick, individuals are merely discouraged because of their self-defeating inferiority complex. Adler was a holiest who thought a person could be understood only as an indivisible unity. He believed that all particular functions were subordinate functions of an individual's goals or style of life. Lifestyle was not synonymous with behavior; behavior can change throughout a person's life whereas the lifestyle remains relatively constant.

To Adler, human beings are creative, self-determined decision-makers who choose the goals they wish to pursue. The "dynamic striving" toward a self-selected goal gives an individual a place in the world. Life has no intrinsic meaning, according to Adler, but each person gives life meaning according to that person's own fashion. Because people grow up in a social environment, they search for significance by attempting to master their environment. If children conceive that they can achieve peace through useful endeavor they will pursue the "useful side of life". If they become discouraged however, they will engage in disturbing behavior in an effort to find their place. Such children will usually use one of four approaches: attention-getting, power-seeking, revenge-taking or declaring defeat.

According to Adler, there are four levels of conviction in a lifestyle. The first is self-concept, the conviction people have about who they are. The second is self-ideal, the conviction of what they should be or are obligated to be to have a place. The third is a picture of the world, not a conviction of self but rather of what the world demands of a person. The last conviction is ethical, a personal code of right and wrong. Inferiority feelings develop when a discrepancy occurs between self and ideal-self convictions.

Since a person's psychological problems emanate from faulty perceptions, learnings, values, and goals, the goal of therapy is one of education or reeducation of those ideas. People need to learn to have faith in themselves, to love, and to trust. Ideally, through psychotherapy their social interest is released so they can become fellow human beings who contribute to and feel a sense of belonging in their world.

Individuals utilize various problem-solving devices to protect their self-esteem, such as compensation, safeguards, excuses, projection, depreciation tendencies, and creating distance. To Adler the concept of the unconscious was not acceptable, so repression and sublimation were irrelevant. Being self-determined, human beings had no room for instincts, drives, libido, or other alleged unconscious motivation.[74]

William Glasser: William Glasser's theory of reality therapy is the focus of responsible behavior. In pursuit of such behavior the "Three R's" must be observed: Face Reality; Do Right; and Be Responsible. According to reality therapy most psychiatric help is sought because of failure to fulfill two needs, love and self-worth. The focus should be on the present, not on the past, and on behavior rather than on feelings.

Individuals must face reality and admit that the past cannot be rewritten. They must accept full responsibility for their present and future behavior. Unconscious motivation is no excuse for misbehavior. What is important is a person's present attempts to succeed and intentions for the future. The therapist helps individuals devise specific plans for their behavior and make a commitment to follow through with their plans.

Human beings have a single most important social need-for identity. That intrinsic need is inherited and transmitted from generation to generation.

The identity one develops comes from interaction with others as well as interaction with oneself. An identity change follows a change in behavior. To change what we are, we must change what we do and undertake new ways of behaving. Reality therapy focuses strongly on helping individuals understand and accept themselves as they are with their own internal limitations and abilities.

The therapist in reality therapy must be personal, encouraging the individual to make a value judgment and plan to alter behavior. Making a commitment to a choice develops maturity. No excuses are accepted for not following through. Positive in approach, the therapist never focuses on punishment, attempting instead to lead a person out of a failure identity. In reality therapy, individuals are assisted in understanding, defining, and clarifying both immediate and long term goals in identifying the ways they hamper their own progress toward goals, and in comparing alternatives.

Of the various secular schools of thought, reality therapy seems to have had the greatest influence on Christian counseling. Its emphasis on responsibility and its attempt to distinguish between right and wrong are commendable; yet in reality therapy morality is relative because it is based on no absolute standard.[75]

According to Transactional Analysis (TA), humans have several basic needs. The first is stroke hunger, the need for another person's time, attention, and physical contact. A second is recognition hunger, which is satisfied when others recognize one's existence. Structure hunger, or what to do with our time, is a third need. Another need is leadership hunger, especially the opportunity of helping others structure their time. Our final need is excitement hunger which is met by structuring time in ways that seem most exciting. Transactional analysis uses a number of terms in a special way. For example, "script" is a life plan, decided on at an early age, through which individuals meet their needs in the world as they see it from the vantage point of their "life position". Script is a life plan containing within its lines the significant things that will happen to a person. The four possible life positions are:

a. I am OK, you are OK.

b. I am OK, you are not OK.

c. I am not OK, you are OK.

d. I am not OK, you are not OK.

The importance of life position is that it helps determine the type of script a person will pursue throughout life. "Games" are a series of transactions occurring on two different levels of communication simultaneously, with an unexpected twist leading to a payoff perhaps a particular feeling, such as guilt, depression, or anger. Three ego states form the basis for structural analysis. The first is "child", which encompasses the feelings, attitudes, and behavior patterns of a child under six. The second ego state is "parent". That state reflects advice and values, the "should" and "should-nots", and is programmed both socially and traditionally. The last state, "adult", is the aspect of ego that responds to reality. "Rackets" are the feelings individuals collect to justify the major actions in their life script.

Transactional analysis is contractual treatment in which patients specify what they expect to achieve in the therapeutic relationship. The therapist accepts or rejects the contract, depending on whether or not the therapist thinks he or she can help. Therapy begins with structural analysis, the identification and delineation of the three ego states in the individual and in others. Structural analysis is followed by transactional analysis, that is, analysis of the ego states from which transactions emanate and the ego states to which actions are directed.

Although influenced by others, the ultimate choice of life script is that of the individual. Individuals choose the script best adapted to the life position already decided on, and the games and rackets that can readily be learned within family injunctions and their own wishes, needs, and desires. The alternative to game playing is an autonomous, self-chosen life pattern that can be changed to a more interesting and rewarding pattern at any time. From a Christian viewpoint, the problem with TA is that without Christ, change is difficult - and no one is really OK.[76]

Behavior is composed of cognitive, motor, and emotional responses and is responsive to both external and internal stimulation. Inappropriate behavior is learned and can be changed systemically. Neurosis is unabated learned behavior. Such maladaptive behavior can be corrected by application of techniques derived from laws of learning.

Behavior therapy emphasizes changes in overt behavior. Direct behavior modification leads to changes in feelings and attitudes. Techniques used in therapy include counterconditioning (for example, replacing anxiety by response that contradicts anxiety), desensitization, participant modeling, aversion therapy, and operant techniques. In operant techniques a person is rewarded for engaging in appropriate behavior and punished for inappropriate behavior. The therapist expects clients to set specific goals to aid in their own treatment.

Behavior modification usually refers to in-patient therapy, whereas behavior therapy refers to out-patient therapy. Positive and negative reinforcement and assertiveness training are parts of behavior modification. Behavior modification works particularly well with phobias and obsessive thinking.

Several problems are inherent in behavior modification, which is most effective with straightforward types of disorders. One question is whether long-term improvement really occurs. Behavior therapists have also been challenged about the questionable ethics of some of their techniques.[77]

Rational-Emotive therapy is active and directive. This school of thought believes that psychological problems are a result of irrational belief systems or patterns of thought. It operates on an A-B-C paradigm. "A" refers to events in a person's life. "B" refers to a person's thought about event "A". "C" represents a person's emotions and behavior as a result of "B". When a highly charged emotional consequence (C) follows an activating event (A), "A" may appear to cause "C". Actually, however, emotional consequences are largely created by "B", the individual's belief system

The goal of therapy is to minimize a person's central self-defeating outlook and help him or her acquire a more realistic, total philosophy of life. Pain may be alleviated in several ways, including diversion, satisfaction of demands, and convincing a person to give up demandingness. Counselees are taught basically how to think - to separate rational from irrational beliefs.

The rational-emotive therapist is informal, active, energetic, and directive. Often a forceful approach is necessary to alter destructive patterns of behavior. Homework assignments and facing and experiencing unpleasant events are part of this therapy. Resistance is usually handled by showing individuals that they are resistant to changing their outlook and behavior because change is difficult and because they prefer a magical solution rather than work to bring change. [78]

Carl Rogers believes that all individuals possess a strong drive toward personal growth, health, and adjustment, which he calls "self-actualization". Tension, anxiety, and defensiveness interfere with basic human drives. If those forces can be reduced or relieved, a person can experience personal growth. Neurotic individuals, according to Rogers, have taken on the values of others. The goal of client-centered therapy is to help people regain contact with their true feelings and values. Increased self-acceptance increases autonomy and reduces the destructive forces of anxiety; thus personal growth occurs.

In client-centered therapy the therapist is the key and needs to be honest, genuine, transparent, and totally accepting. According to Rogers, the growth potential of individuals is released in a relationship where a helping person is experiencing and communicating realness, caring, and a deeply sensitive, nonjudgmental understanding. The client-centered approach is applicable to any relationship where persons want to understand and be understood and are willing to reveal themselves to some degree.

Client-centered therapists must have an unconditional, positive regard for the other person. They must accept the client as a person regardless of how socially unacceptable that person's behavior and feelings may be. Therapists must possess empathy and must try to understand as clearly as possible the feelings of the client.

Finally, therapists must be genuine, able to be "themselves" in a session and express their thoughts and feelings without pretension. Client-centered therapy is especially effective for individuals with a low self-image.[79]

Analytical psychotherapy is an attempt to create a relationship between the conscious and the unconscious. Carl Jung believed that all products of the unconscious are symbolic and therefore to be interpreted as guiding messages. The basis of analysis should be experiencing, not merely understanding intellectually. The main work of the analytic process is interpretation, particularly dream analysis. Jung believed dreams to be unconscious messages expressed in symbolic form.

According to Jung a person has several parts, the first being the ego, or center of the consciousness. It is the sum total of thoughts, ideas, feelings, memories, and sensory perception. Another part is the personal unconscious, which is everything that has been repressed during a person's development. One also possesses a non-personal unconscious, which includes archetypes and inborn psychic predispositions to perception, emotion, and behavior. Jung refers to the conscious and unconscious together as the psyche.

Another quality found in a person is the person's, or actor's mask. It is often worn as a barrier between the inner psychological life and the outside world. The shadow, or "other side", is all that a person would not like to be, the compensatory side of a person's conscious ego. Human beings also possess an animus or anima. The anima in men and the animus in women are an individual's counter-sex parts. Finally, Jung considers the self to be the inherent psychic predisposition to experience wholeness or meaning in life. This urge toward wholeness is the state of being what one was meant to become. Among the contributions made by Jung to psychology are the word-association test and the terms introvert and extrovert.[80]

Gestalt experiential therapy seeks to create experiences that increase a person's self-awareness. Frederick Perls believed that people are kept from reaching their potential because they do not have the opportunity to discover fully who they are. Individuals are responsible for their own decisions and actions, and cannot blame society, parents, or past experiences for their problems. When individuals can accept themselves to the fullest extent possible, they can overcome conflicts within their personalities so that psychological growth occurs.

According to gestalt therapy, people rarely tap the potential within themselves or between themselves and others. Our awareness is usually directed to a few areas that are consistent with our sense of identity, and then all experience is funneled through that concept of ourselves. Limited self-concepts constrict awareness and inhibit experiences, so that awareness is not allowed freedom. Gestalt therapy attempts to counteract that limitation by broadening experiences. [81]

Conclusion

All of these secular schools/models have a number of limitations, the first being that they come with the general philosophy that man evolved, and they have no standard of authority. For Christians, authority rests in the Bible alone as the Word of God. Without this absolute standard, any school of thought is handicapped. Second, most of the schools are concerned only with treatment of psychological matters, not with spiritual matters. Third, will power is often insufficient in affecting full and complete change, which must be an act of God. It is imperative to realize that therapy, even in its utopia cannot change a human being. It is the understanding and acceptance of one's unique self that an individual can see permanent change in his/her life by allowing God to effect that change by doing the following:

a. Understanding of one's unique self
b. Surrendering to the Lord Jesus Christ and His plan for our lives.
c. Having a willingness to surrender the ungodly ways of meeting our needs and replacing them with methods which are conducive to the Holy Scriptures.

Christians can rely on God to help them when they need additional strength. Some schools of thought completely ignore the premise that human beings are basically selfish. "Self-actualization" requires the opposing premise, that human beings are basically good. Christians recognize that they must rely on God and His Word to change their lives. A Christian counselor thus has a resource found in none of the secular schools.

Introduction to Legal and Ethical Practice

Legal and ethical scholars are concerned with the preciseness of their language. Clinicians, as well, spend a great part of their time splitting linguistic hairs over the relative merits of using one phase over another, attempting to cultivate an appreciation for the verbal options available in describing one's thoughts and feelings. Therapists and counselors could even be described as "language coaches" whose principal function is to promote greater internal control, self-responsibility, rationality, and clarity by the use of positive, self-enhancing images, metaphors, descriptors of innermost thoughts.

Ethics is concerned with questions that have no ultimate answers yet are important to planning one's life, justifying one's activities, and deciding what one ought to do. More so than psychology and other social sciences that attempt to describe human behavior, ethical philosophy is concerned with evaluating human conduct. Ethics, values, and morality are an intrinsic part of therapy practice. In the therapeutic relationship, the very concept of influence is a moral issue.

During the past few decades, the craft of counseling and psychotherapy has attained a prominent place in Western society: "Its professors and practitioners, once contemptuously regarded as eccentrics mumbling arcane obscenities at the fringe of medicine, have advanced from relative obscurity to chairs of eminence and couches of opulence in the finest universities and neighborhoods in the Western world" (London, 1964, p. v.).[82]

Chapter XVIII
Perspectives on Ethical Practice

All professionals have moral codes, general rules to guide behavior. For therapists, as well as physicians, and lawyers, have rules of conduct to guide them so that all may flourish. Thus, a profession, much more than a knowledge discipline, is concerned with the issues of sanction, legitimacy, setting, knowledge, and methods of practice or intervention. All professions have ethical codes and standards in one form or another. These standards reflect the professional activity of the therapist.

Many people believe that ethical standards for professional groups are designed to protect the public from charlatans and incompetents. While they may sometimes have such an effect, that is not the only reason for their existence. More often they are designed to protect the profession from three main dangers. First, ethical standards are designed to protect the profession from the government. All professions desire autonomy and seek to avoid interference and regulation by lawmakers. They would rather regulate themselves through professional codes or standards rather than risk regulations from legislative bodies. Second, ethical standards protect the professions from the self-destruction of internal bickering. It is unethical to criticize a professional colleague or to entice his clients to leave him. This standard enables therapists to live in harmony with one another. Finally, ethical standards are designed to protect the therapist from the public. If he behaves within the code, he has some protection if he is sued for malpractice (Fish, 1973).

Much of what the therapist does and why he does it cannot be understood outside a context of human values. Psychotherapy is certainly a value-laden activity. We intervene directly in the lives of our clients, often helping them change their behavior, their standards, and their view of themselves.

Statutory laws dealing with such matters as licensure, malpractice, and privacy vary greatly from state to state and in some states are nonexistent. In 1985, for example, while all states had laws governing the private practice of psychology, only ten states had laws distinguishing between counseling and psychology and regulating the private practice of counseling. Within the past few decades, the helping professions have gained a prominent position in American society. Counseling and psychotherapy, along with other helping crafts, are not only sanctioned by the state but also supported by a public that expects therapists to provide mental health care to large segments of society.

The theory is a systematic way of organizing a body of knowledge into meaningful perspective. Patterns of behavior and thought are simplified and structured so as to provide guidelines for action and make sense of complex phenomena. There is, of course, a distinction between the theories espoused by a therapist and those actually used in practice. Perhaps more than a single theory, we are dealing with a collection of theoretical conceptions.

Ethics is a branch of philosophy that is concerned primarily with how and why people make moral decisions (Daubner and Daubner, 1972). Law, whether enacted by a legislature or established by a court, is designed to govern the affairs of man. Laws tell us what we can and cannot do; and if we do something that is prohibited, and get caught, laws tell us what is likely to happen to us afterward. Ethical judgments do not enjoy the degree of precision that legal issues do in deciding what is a correct act and what is not. Ethics covers the realm of conduct not covered under the law. Traditionally, the roles of law and ethics as governing rules were both contained in religious bodies.

There is not necessarily a perfect correlation between what one believes and how one acts. A therapist may genuinely believe that his professional service is a good thing and that economically disadvantaged people as well as his affluent clients should have the opportunity to benefit from his service.

The proponents of the self-realization approach to ethics view man as an innately good creature who has the ability to grow naturally into a moral being and to make ethical decisions that are good and right. Abraham Maslow (1908-1970) constructed what can be considered the most complete and relevant self-realization theory of our time. Maslow, perhaps more than any other twentieth-century theoreticians, was responsible for the growth in humanistic science.

Eric Fromm (1900-1980), the neo psychoanalytical theorist, also contributed to humanistic ethics in his book (Man for Himself, 1947). Fromm based morality on man's intrinsic ability to reason and postulated that the sources of norms for ethical conduct are found in human nature, in man's powers to discern good from bad or right from wrong.

Running parallel with the humanist school is the existentialist approach to morality. Existentialism as a philosophy that views experience as the core of meaningful existence was first expounded in Europe by such writers as Soren Kierkegaard, Paul Tillich, and Jean-Paul Sartre. Among contemporary Americans, Rollo May (1958-1967, 1983), Carl Rogers (1951, 1961), Dugald Arbuckle (1965), and Irvin Yalom (1980) are exemplary champions of the existentialist cause as it relates to counseling and psychotherapy.

The moral development point of view is more an outgrowth of psychology than of traditional philosophy.

On the basis of longitudinal and cross-cultural studies of children in a dozen countries as well as in his own experimental "Cluster School", Kohlberg concludes that teachers and counselors can best promote ethical behavior by (1) exposing people to higher stages of moral reasoning; (2) presenting irreconcilable ethical conflicts that lead to dissatisfaction with current, more primitive levels of thinking; and (3) creating a therapeutic atmosphere that permits open dialogue. Ideally, these conditions may be generated within the context of therapy sessions as well.

The regulations of all therapist behavior are based entirely on a belief system concerning what is right for a particular client. Since the core of the therapist's system of what is right and wrong, good and bad, effective and ineffective, appropriate and inappropriate is based on a philosophical ethical system, this value must be developed to optimal levels.

Most people are not totally proficient in all areas of ethical functioning. There is much work to be done to achieve greater ethical responsibility. The ground rule for the practitioner is: If one has a specific, responsible rationale for a given behavior, can defend it as justifiable under the circumstances, and the results turn out favorably, one is in the clear. If, however, the result turns out poorly and somebody complains or files suit, the same action may be construed as irresponsible, unethical, incompetent, or illegal. By committing himself to upgrade his ethical behavior and working diligently to assess his current levels of functioning, desired goals, and courses of action necessary to meet moral responsibilities to himself, his client, and his profession, the therapist can refine his competencies and protect himself against outside interference, and legal suits.[83]

Chapter XIX
Therapy Legal Regulations

Contrary to popular opinion, law is not cut and dried, definite and certain, or clear and precise. To paraphrase Foster (1975), law invariably expresses compromise; it seeks to recognize, reconcile, and delimit competing claims and interests, in accordance with the predominant values of a given place and time. Law provides few definite answers, and almost every rule has its exceptions. Moreover, there is no general body of law covering the helping professions. There are few laws dealing with counseling in schools and community settings, particularly when the counselor has no psychiatric training and holds no license to practice psychology or psychotherapy.

The therapist structures the relationship with the client by defining the helping situation - by explaining what therapy is and what it is not. Roy and Pine (1982) believe that therapists should explain that they do not have solutions to the client's problems but will help the client search for appropriate solutions. The client has a right to expect he will be treated as a human being and not as an object of passing importance (Foster, 1975). Legally, the therapist has a duty to communicate to the client an honest representation of his skills and methods, along with the conditions of therapy, fees, appointment schedules, and special obligations of both therapist and client. The understanding that develops during the first contacts becomes, in effect, an unwritten contract.

The most usual circumstance for termination of treatment occurs when therapist and client mutually agree (1) that the client is "cured" or perhaps has reached desired goals, or will not benefit from further treatment, and (2) that the client will be referred to another professional.

People who enter therapy often discuss intimate and personal details and concerns. Clients have a right to expect that these private revelations will be treated confidentially and that the therapist will not disclose information that might bring shame or ridicule to the client. The issues of confidentiality bring into sharp focus the nature of the therapist's loyalty to the client, the employing institution, society, the profession, and himself. Ethical codes, statutes, and court decisions have established the principle that people are entitled to keep some things private. Only under proper legal safeguards may they be required to reveal what they would prefer to keep secret.

The special relationship between a therapist and his client creates a duty to use special skill and due care in treatment. The therapist represents himself by means of words, by exchanging ideas, and by sharing feelings, and these actions are part of the treatment process.

Traditionally, in commitment proceedings and criminal cases, courts seeking expert testimony on a defendant's behavior or mental health relied primarily on a therapist with a medical degree.

Recently, however, psychologists have also become generally recognized as experts who can draw inferences about human behavior that is outside the experience of the ordinary juror (Pacht and Solomon, 1973).

A high percentage of counselors and psychotherapists work in institutions, schools, colleges, hospitals, youth agencies, and mental health centers. Some of the information used by institutions is personal and intimate, and often used improperly. Some institutions, schools and colleges in particular, have consistently misused information about students, and in the process, have invaded the individual's privacy. They have released information to other schools, employers, the police and the FBI without permission or, even the knowledge of the student or their parents. The legal implications of the use of this information, including oral and written statements about a client, involve matters of personal rights, possible defamation, libel and slander, and privileged information.

Therapists and institutions have a right to collect whatever information is specially and initially necessary to carry out their mission. They also have both a legal and an ethical responsibility to safeguard the rights and privacy of their clients. They must also be able to document what is said with more than opinions, beliefs, and professional hunches.

Malpractice is generally defined as damage to another person as a result of negligence. The concept is based on several ancient laws which held that a person who injures another person must give him something to compensate for that injury. In the present era, the injured party brings a legal action against the other person or his property, in an effort to set right the injury done to him.

Three conditions must be proved in malpractice litigation: (1) The defendant had a duty to the plaintiff; (2) the defendant's conduct constituted negligence or improper action; 3) there was a causal relationship between that negligence and the damage alleged by the plaintiff (Burgum and Anderson, 1975). The term "damage" refers to losses suffered in money, body, or mind. "Negligence" is defined as a departure from usual practice; that is, accepted standards were not followed, and due care was not exercised.

When compared with lawsuits brought against physicians, malpractice actions brought against counselors and psychotherapists are infrequent.

The best safeguard against malpractice is professional and personal honesty. Openness in communications with clients and a demonstrated interest in the welfare of those being helped are good defenses against charges of malpractice. The legal dimensions of counseling and psychotherapy are not yet clearly defined. Statute law and case law leave many questions unanswered and provide few guidelines on the specifics of therapy and the legal process. Professional associations have given minimal attention to the legal aspects of counseling and psychotherapy. However, there is evidence that events highlighting the legal vulnerability of therapists and the trend toward accountability may stimulate positive professional action.

One criterion of a profession is that it be self-disciplining and self-licensing. Established professionals - whether antique merchants, hairdressers, or therapists - developed standards and policies that, to some degree at least, control entry into the profession, prescribe training standards, and establish procedures and requirements for licensing or certification. Professionals also develop ethical codes, which outline standards of service, describe members' relationships with each other and with the general public, and spell out appropriate and inappropriate behavior of members.

Two organizations that have developed comprehensive standards for counseling and psychotherapy are the American Association for Counseling and Development, and the American Psychological Association. The American Psychiatric Association and the American Medical Association have also given considerable attention to standards for the practice of psychiatry. Since the practice of psychiatry, however, requires a medical license, the regulatory process is somewhat different from those of counseling and psychology.

Counseling in schools differs from other specialties in several significant ways. The first of these differences is in the training and experience requirements. The skills demanded of teachers are not necessarily those demanded of counselors, and competence in teachers has little bearing on the competence required for effective counseling. We maintain that the primary task of any professional using the title of "counselor" is counseling and furthermore, that the counseling task has been clearly defined. Unfortunately, many jobs and activities described as counselors are at best quasi-administrative or clerical and at worst a fraud and misrepresentation of the profession.

To some degree every profession is subject to analogous professional problems and criticism. Few professions can function to the satisfaction of everyone, and each has its share of critics and detractors. Such criticism can be useful in encouraging self-examination and is essential in stimulating improvement in professional practice. Considerable impetus for more comprehensive and definitive standards emerged from APA Division 17 (Counseling Psychology) and Division 22 (Rehabilitation Psychology) in the 1960's. In 1962 and 1963, a committee from Counseling Psychology prepared a comprehensive outline of standards for rehabilitation counselors. The APA standards provide a generic description of psychologists and require that the person offering services hold a doctorate and present evidence of appropriate professional experience. In 1975 the APA Council of Representatives created a standing Committee on Standards for Providers of Psychological Services. The charge for the committee is to review and revise the standards so that they remain timely and workable.

Many practitioners in related professions feel that they are doing psychotherapy in the formal sense and are involved in developing and implementing standards for self-governance and professional autonomy. The National Association of Social Workers and the American Association for Marriage and Family Therapy, for example, have attempted to improve the profession by setting standards for the training, licensure, and conduct of members. The American Association for Marriage and Family Therapy (1982) has developed comprehensive standards for persons in this counseling specialty.

Ethical standards or codes represent yet another way that professionals attempt to govern and discipline themselves. Ethical standards deal with proper professional conduct and serve as guidelines for the therapist's work with clients. In addition, ethical standards help the therapist deal with such questions as, "What modes of conduct are favorable or unfavorable to service for this client?" and, "What conduct is required in this situation?"

The adoption of ethical standards and the knowledge of ethical principles do not in themselves solve ethical problems of therapists. However, ethical standards generally discourage the practice of therapy by unqualified persons; even so, some professional organizations accept members mainly on the basis of their interest and willingness to pay dues. There should be a direct relationship between ethical responsibilities and legal principles that is applicable to therapy.

Professional licensure laws define the practice of a profession and restrict functions to those who meet specified qualifications. A licensing law usually forbids use of a title - psychologist, for example - by an unqualified person. Licensure certification for the private practice of counseling by counselors not credentialed as psychologists or psychiatrists has emerged recently as a major professional issue. Many counselors maintain that counseling is a unique mental health profession.

The private practices of counseling and legal recognition of counseling as separate from psychology are related issues that have generated considerable conflict between psychologists and counselors in some localities. During the past decade, ten states have enacted licensure laws for counselors. Clearly, the advocates of strong licensure laws for counselors and psychotherapists have advanced several good and sufficient reasons for the legislation. At the present time control of the helping professions is divided among the training institutions, the states handling licensure and certification, and professional associations.

Human interaction is guided by the value and personal philosophy of the parties involved. Values and philosophy determine how we react to experiences in life, how we plan our life goals, and the manner in which we attempt to achieve these goals. Few people act independently of their values, even when these values are unclear and vaguely defined. Perry (1974) describes values as attitudes that influence the way people respond to ideas, events, and objects they encounter. He believes that values have no objective status; "it is not a quality of the world we experience; rather, a value exists only in the eye of the beholder." The therapist must develop an awareness, not only of his own values but also of the value structure of others. All people have beliefs about how things ought to be or how they would like them to be. Values lie largely in the realm of ethics and ethical behavior.

Some of the most dramatic changes of this century have occurred in rules for personal conduct. Several religious leaders and fundamentalist Christian groups around the country are uneasy about these changes. If it is acknowledged that there is no such thing as a value-free therapy, then the value contracts between therapists and society at large may become more marked. Evidence presented by Gross and Kahn (1983) suggests that the philosophy of therapists is markedly different from that of the fundamentalists.

There was a time when a therapist was not supposed to deal with values, and any suggestion that values should be imposed on clients was considered not only coercive but anti-therapeutic. It is now believed that therapists should not have only mild values or that expression of beliefs or attitudes are prima facie wrong. On the contrary, often a therapist must take a consistent and firm position during the process of ministering to his clients. It is not made clear altogether about the role of the therapist in the values area, but is certain that he cannot ignore it. Several questions have been raised in relation to a therapist's obligations to both the client and society.[84]

Chapter XX
Ethical Conflicts

In our democratic society, people are, of course, free to act in any way they choose as long as they do not overstep legal bounds or (irritate someone in a position of power). But, in addition, individuals especially professionals are expected to exercise this freedom in a responsible manner. Although laws are established and ethical codes are standardized to help regulate acceptable behavior, the enforcement of these rules is virtually impossible. Most of the members of the helping professions are competent, honest, ethical, and dedicated. A few, however, do not feel compelled to live up to any external standard except for the accumulation of financial resources and personal gain. Incompetent therapists who must resort to disguises and professional games are fortunately relatively few compared to the large number of ethical and effective professionals. There is no profession more potentially useful or devastating than psychotherapy, its effects and outcomes are subtle, disguised, and often invisible, even to the client. The therapist does not have at his disposal a thermometer or an X-ray to measure the extent or intensity of the difficulty, nor does he have a chemical antidote or mechanical apparatus to make the symptoms disappear and restore tranquil and effective functioning to the client. He must rely on his skill, knowledge, and commitment to helping. In short, he must use the self as an instrument of treatment. It is important to look at ethical practices from the perspective of effects on the client. The goal then, is not to become a perfect, fully functioning human being who always acts ethically and responsibly but an individual willing to refine techniques, to grow professionally and personally, and, more often than not, to act in an ethical and competent manner. The belief that it is unethical and counterproductive to engage in a sexual affair or emotional involvement with a client is not universal. There are therapists who genuinely believe and practice the notion that sexual involvement with a client may be beneficial. Regardless of any conceivable benefits from sexual encounters, it is incomprehensible that the possible side effects, problems, and complications could ever justify this activity.

Therapists are often unaware that they may be developing dependencies in their clients. Instead of providing opportunities for clients to make decisions in their own lives, therapists may continually give advice and offer what they believe to be the solution to problems. A key issue for therapists is to critically assess whether they are promoting such dependencies in clients by failing to help them become independent or by seeing them longer than necessary. The therapist's ultimate goal must be to promote independence in clients.

The issue of therapeutic deception has come to the forefront as structural family therapy, in, Minuchin and Fishman, 1981. Certainly, no matter how we justify or rationalize our actions, we are lying whenever we trick clients out of their symptoms, whenever we take on pretend roles, whenever we operate paradoxically. "The question in this situation is not so much a question of whether the therapist is telling a lie but whether he is behaving unethically" (Haley, 1976, p.203). In a therapeutic relationship, a therapist's self-disclosures can effectively promote the therapeutic relationship, illustrate a principle, model how effectively a human being can act in a certain situation, and show that the therapist is a person, not just a role. These are all examples that help with self-disclosures. There is a fine line between an effective self-disclosure, and a self-disclosure that may be used, just because the therapist likes to hear himself talk, wanting the client's approval, or one who attempts to use therapy time to meet his own needs.

Imposing one's own values and beliefs on a client is another unethical behavior that is commonly engaged in but rarely questioned (Ajze, 1973). Do therapists have the right to train their clients into duplicate selves? Admittedly, therapy is an influencing interaction between a trained expert and a recipient of professional services; but who should decide what behavior needs to be changed, and in what direction? If the client is to be the expert in declaring goals, it is the therapist's responsibility, then, to help the client reach them? It would seem to be necessary and desirable to withhold our values from clients. Values are the components of our personal code of action. They allow us to select therapeutic options based on a schema of what is basically good or bad for people.

Confidentiality is both a legal and an ethical problem for helping professionals. Current professional literature deals at length with such matters as privacy, privileged communication, confidentiality, records, and use of test information. All clients wonder what is expected of them the first time they come into the office for an interview. They wonder whether the therapist is trustworthy and what he will do with the private information that he is privileged to hear.

There are several conditions that may contribute to incompetent and, or, unethical behavior. They may be; faulty, or inadequate training, lack of skill, poor judgment, laziness, and lack of commitment to acceptable professional practices, these may all lead to incompetent services.

Certain therapeutic procedures, such as hypnosis, paradoxical directives, behavior modification, biofeedback, sex therapy, psychopharmacology, group work, and several applications of therapy in the media involve additional ethical principles to govern their use.

Group work is the only therapeutic activity in which other clients, who are themselves in need of help, help serve as therapists (Gazada, Duncan, and Sisson, 1971). Clients have no therapeutic training and are not guided by any professional code of ethics or obligated to honor privileged communication; yet they regularly engage in confronting their peers, interpreting their behavior, and providing a form of counseling. Group counseling also can be seen as an oppressive influence, for example, when it deradicalizes children to conform to the status quo (Jeffries, 1973). Children are socialized into roles that take away their individuality and mold them into obedient citizens who follow rules without question.

Group practitioners experience other ethical difficulties in their role. While they are influential and powerful, they have less control over the proceedings than in individual sessions (Kettler 1983), verbal abuse is more likely (Corey and others, 1982), and leaders sometimes have little training and few qualifications to deal with critical incidents that occur (Gumaer, 1982).

The group leaders, who represent themselves as "educational consultants," are not required to have any skills or training or to meet the criteria that apply to professional practitioners. Even hairdressers and barbers need a license to work with the human head, yet encounter group leaders are exempt from regulations when dealing with what is in the human head (Peters, 1973).

Every effort should be made on the part of the group leader to ensure that only stable individuals are included. Brief case histories, intake interviews, and psychological testing are often helpful. Positive experiences can best be assured through a democratic and safe atmosphere, a well-trained leader, and protection of clients from coercion and abuse.

All the ethical concerns of group work are compounded in the treatment of multiple family members who go home together after the session. Still other ethical issues make the marketing and practice of family therapy especially difficult. Confidentiality issues are certainly more complex, especially with regard to handling family secrets.

The helping professional can attain ethical respectability, by being open, specific, and honest about the nature of therapeutic services, the goals of treatment, and what is likely to happen in the sessions. Therapists who engage in professional services without specifying what the client is likely to get for his money are asking persons to follow a mysterious open-ended journey without any notion of where they are going, how they will get there, and how long it will take.

Restrictions on advertising and public promotion rest on the historical conception that professionals are devoted to public service rather than to making money and that overt marketing tarnishes the profession's image. According to Goldberg (1977), the client's rights can best be preserved by attention to concepts of equity and balance in the therapeutic relationship. Roles, goals, and responsibilities should be clarified. It is the therapist's responsibility not only to deliver expert therapeutic help but also to describe accurately what he can and cannot do for the public. At the very minimum, prospective clients have a right to know about the therapist's training, qualifications, fees, specialties, and limitations, as well as his conceptions of how therapy will help. It is through the honest and precise labeling of their services that therapists establish true credibility with their clients, their colleagues, and themselves.[85]

Chapter XXI
Ethical Principles and Individual Conduct

Most therapists, philosophically at least, subscribe to the basic ethical standards and principles of their profession. In a like manner, most of us support and obey the law, and we generally accept the need for social rules to govern human conduct. But we do not do so blindly or without question. Consequently, counselors have problems with credentialing, and ethical questions surrounding program accreditation, licensure, and certification.

The American Association for Counselors and Development, through its accreditation unit, has approved 28 of 424 counselor education programs since the inceptions of this unit in 1981. Minimal requirements for accreditation are that programs train counselors at a two-year master's level. Ten states now license counselors, some at the master's level. The major arguments for program accreditation and individual practitioner licensure are program improvement and protection for the public. But given the fact of hundreds of programs training counselors at the master's level, and thousands of licensed professional counselors now ready to engage in private practice, it is doubtful whether the AACD's efforts have yet been productive of greater professionalization or public protection.

Ethical codes or standards provide helpful guidelines for the professional behavior of counselors and psychotherapists. By the same logic, laws enacted by democratically elected legislators or legal decisions issued by courts represent an essential social arrangement and cannot be violated with impunity.

Rules governing the professional behavior of therapists are necessary to the continued existence of the profession. Moreover, the therapists who accept the status provided by the profession have a responsibility for adhering to the principles set forth in the profession's code of ethics. We may question the specific meanings of a code and debate its application, but if fundamental principles are ignored, then we are lost, because we have no basis for making judgments and no way of knowing whether we have behaved properly or improperly.[86]

Chapter XXII
Family Law

Because of the increased need of service involvement, there is an increased need for human services professionals to know the law. More and more professionals are being called as expert witnesses. Effective testimony implies familiarity with the legal issues in question and the process by which they will be decided. Becoming involved in the legal system is not a mere matter of introduction. It is necessary to make adaptations. In point of fact, human service professionals, as contrasted to professionals from other disciplines, may find movement into the legal system difficult because of their philosophy and their methods.

Over half of the civil filings in the United States involve some aspect of family law, usually divorce (Hennessey, 1980). The decisions in many of these cases are among the most difficult that judges are called on to make, because the major considerations are essentially non-legal and require the expertise of human services professionals trained in mental health services. Because human services professionals are so important to the proper functioning of the family law systems, they need to understand the basic concept of family law. Under the English common law, marriage was a contract between a man and a woman that imposed on both parties the legal duties defined by the state (Strickman, 1982). The precise nature of the contemporary martial contract and the role of the state in the fulfillment of that contract is currently undergoing changes (Shultz, 1982).

The Supreme Court has characterized a person's marital choice as a fundamental right: "The freedom to marry has long been recognized as one of the vital personal rights essential to the orderly pursuit of happiness by free men" (Loving v. Virginia, 388 U.S., 1, 12 (1977)). According to Krouse (1977), a prenuptial agreement is a contract made by a couple before their marriage in order to modify certain legal results that would otherwise occur. Most states require that the prenuptial contract be in written form. Generally, prenuptial agreements that concern the transfer of property before the marriage are considered valid, although there may be federal tax consequences.

Although the practice of living with someone of the opposite sex without being married is an old one, it appears to be a more common phenomenon today, both in, the United States and in Europe (Glendon, 1980).

The remedies available to an abused spouse are often limited. The recourse normally remains to be; at the time of the assault, the abused spouse can call the police, and may be able to press charges. Also, a restraining order may be granted, a legal order restricting the rights of one or both parties.

According to Krause (1977), the creation of the parent-child relationship encompasses four topics: abortion, legitimacy, paternity, and adoption. The most important case on the subject of abortion is the Supreme Court decision in Roe v. Wade 410 U.S. 113 (1973), in which the court examined the state's interest in regulating abortion. A second topic relating to the establishment of the parent-child relationship is legitimacy. A legitimate child is one "who has full legal relationship with both of its parents" (Krause, 1977, p. 119). States employ a variety of proceedings to determine the issue of paternity. In some states paternity is settled in a civil proceeding; in other states it is dealt with as an adjunct to a criminal proceeding.

Clark (1968, p. 602) defines adoption as "the legal process by which a child acquires parents other than his natural parents, and parents acquire a child other than a natural child."

In recent years there has been an increase in the number of instances where only one member of the married couple is the natural parent of their child. In the case of artificial insemination of the mother from a donor who is not the husband, the child probably will be presumed to be legitimate, since it was born to a married woman. Although some courts have not reached this conclusion, one court, at least, has held that artificial insemination does not constitute adultery if the husband consents to the procedure (People v. Sorensen, 66 Cal. Rptr.7.437 p. 2nd 495 (1968)).

If a court finds that a parent abused or neglected his or her children, several options are available to it (Krause, 1977). First, it may remove the children from the custody of the parents, temporarily or permanently. Second, it may appoint a temporary or permanent guardian who takes responsibility for the child's wellbeing. The question of when the state should become involved in parent-child relations is a difficult one.

Not all marriages are successful. Indeed, recent statistics indicate that about 11 percent of all men and about 19 percent of all women who have ever been married are divorced or separated (U.S. Bureau of the Census, 1981). There are over 1.1 million divorces annually, affecting approximately the same number of children (U.S. Bureau of Census, 1981). In contrast to marriage, which is governed by relatively simple administrative procedures, divorce depends on more complex questions of fact and requires more complicated judicial mechanisms (Strickman, 1982).

The division of property after a divorce is very complex. In most divorces with children involved, custody is not an issue initially because the divorcing parents agree that one or the other should have custody and the judge accepts this agreement. Problems with child custody often arise later, however, so that child custody is best seen as a continuing ongoing concern, rather than a one-time determination.

A problem in applying the child's best interests test, is that many of the factors require judges to assess the quality of the child's interaction and adjustments and to decide how much weight should be attached to each of the interactions.

How children react to the divorce is relevant to the law in that any problems the children experience may affect the judgments concerning modification of custody. There are clear guidelines governing child support awards after a divorce. The kinds of factors considered by judges, however, relate to the income, resources, and services of the two parties. Although the obligation of child support is difficult to enforce in an ongoing family except in cases of gross default, there are enforcement mechanisms available if the parties live apart (Krause, 1977).

Family law is one of the fastest-changing areas of the law as society changes.[87]

Chapter XXIII
Rights of Institutionalized Patients

Concern for the welfare of the mentally ill has not been a routine characteristic of our past (Barton and Sanborn, 1978; Dingman, 1976; Halpren, 1976). On the contrary, the mentally ill were historically either ignored or badly treated by a superstitious and cruel society. Concerns that treatment in a mental hospital may be harmful and dehumanizing have not been limited to popular literature but have also found expression through recent litigation and legislation.

The mental health professional who works in a mental hospital must sometimes feel, particularly when touched by the effects of legal scrutiny into the care of the inpatient, that this world is often irrational and unfair. The patient who is placed in a psychiatric hospital will routinely suffer massive feelings of loss and separation (Goffman, 1961; Rosenhan, 1973). Life in a mental hospital, although meant to be a restorative experience, presents a variety of potential physical and psychological dangers to the patient.

The very fact of being housed in an institution causes a loss of fundamental and constitutionally protected rights.

Constitutional theories suggested for use in mental hospital actions include claims that hospital practices have violated the Fourteenth Amendment's equal protection clause or the Eighth Amendment's prohibition against cruel and unusual punishment. Procedural due process is a fluid concept. There is no single correct or absolute method of decision making.

Courts and legislatures have responded to the recognition that mental health inpatients merit procedural due process protections with two separate maneuvers: (1) legal efforts, particularly by the courts, to carve out or define situations that clearly raise the need for procedural due process; (2) new methods of hospital decision making, including the creation of alternate forums and the provision of advocates to uphold the interests of the patients. Two main rationales have been used to support the state's mental health activities. The government has justified these activities on the notion that it acts out of duty to provide protection and care for those unable to be self-sufficient.

The courts and state legislatures have found due process protections to be necessary in a variety of treatment-related situations. In general, however, these decision-making situations can be classified as either treatment decisions or as decisions that will change the patient's status. The due process protections provided for those who face involuntary commitment do very often include the right to timely notice, the right to a hearing before an impartial fact finder, the right to assess the reliability of evidence through cross-examination or exclusion, and the right to counsel.

If a patient refuses consent or is unable to give informed consent to a hazardous procedure, then review by a court or an ethics committee clearly seems warranted. Patients can, of course, refuse all forms of treatment, and when a patient refuses some forms of treatment, such as psychotherapy, there is typically little real controversy. After all, a therapist would have little success in trying to force unwilling patients to reveal intimate information about themselves.

The clear principle that arises from the transfer cases, when this becomes necessary, is that due process protections are required when the patient is to be placed in a more restrictive environment. But how can a hospital be sure that a transfer represents a move to a more or less restrictive environment? Furthermore, if all deprivations require due process to the extent of the deprivation, must the hospital create a balance between the extent of due process and the nature of specific environmental changes?

Many hospital programs fail to provide sufficient periods of activity for patients. The hospital facilities should also offer privacy to patients. Legal review of the facilities and treatment of the inpatients will continue to effect hospital practices. Specifically, we can expect changes in advocacy forms used to advance patients' interests and in the very conceptualization that underlies our view of mental health treatment. Perhaps the simplest safeguard for patient rights is to allow patients an active and effective participation in determining their hospital treatment. While depending on patients to be their own advocate has a variety of positive features, there are also drawbacks. Perhaps the most serious drawback to allowing patients to serve as their own advocates, without additional help, is that they may experience pressure to conform to the wishes of the hospital staff. The human rights committee is another method of providing protection and advocacy for the inpatient.

There is concern that legal advocates in general and the courts in particular have now come to play an inappropriate role in the treatment of the patient.[88]

Chapter XXIV
Professional Responsibilities and Liabilities

The relationship established between the client or patient and the human service professional is vested with many features that set it apart from all other human relationships. Foremost, the entire relationship is devoted, at least ostensibly, to promoting the welfare of the client.

The professional should be the last person to object to a requirement of informed consent. If anything, the professional should reach to the maximum allowed by public policy to ensure that the service recipient does, in fact, understand and consent to the treatment being offered. In addition to a right to treatment, the courts have spoken decisively in favor of a constitutional right to refuse any treatment. Because of the patient's right to refuse treatment, the professional is, in effect, "stripped of authority" to force individuals to submit to psychological interventions, and therefore, must deal with individuals committed to institutions in a manner as he does with any other individual.

In human services, the client's communication is protected by two types of law; confidentiality and privileged communication (DeKraai and Sales, 1982). Although confidentiality is endorsed by the constitutional right to privacy, as such, confidentiality has to be reasonably expected.

The legal system has established means for opening the previously privileged communications to the eyes and ears of those seeking justice. The professional cannot refuse to cooperate with a subpoena on the grounds that the psychotherapeutic process will be contradicted by the therapist's speaking out.

The courts have held that professionals have a "limited property right" in their records, such as test protocols. This means that if a client wants all records destroyed, for instance, to avoid discovery by a party - opponent in an approaching legal action, the professional does not have to comply with the demand.

The professional is entitled to charge a reasonable fee for any activity associated with the legal proceedings. Information given because of a statutory requirement or a court order removes the professional from any kind of liability for alleged breach of confidentiality.

Malpractice constitutes a breach of professional responsibility. The foundation for a legal action is a violation of an established standard of care for the particular professional service, with the outcome being damage to the client. Traditionally, the standard of care for human services practice was based on what other practitioners in the same geographical community would do under the circumstances.

The four dimensions of the human services relationship are; informed consent, privileged communication, and the duty to warn. Professional malpractices constitute the core of legal concerns Vis a Vis practice. Both the client and the professional can benefit when the existence of these dimensions is openly acknowledged very early in the therapeutic relationship. Some professionals are hesitant to talk to their clients about the inherent duty to breach confidentiality in order to ensure the safety and welfare of all persons, but such a possible breach must be confronted. [89]

Conclusion

In the classic sense, ethics is a very important principle of moral conduct that influences a person's behavior. A written code of ethics sets the standards for practice and rules that govern members of a professional group. Even in our morally bankrupt society, clients want to know that their counselor operates on a higher standard of conduct. Fortunately for Christian counselors, we already have the highest standard of ethics, it's the ethics modeled by Christ during His public ministry on earth. As we counsel and manage our business according to Scriptural principles, we are able to meet, and, even exceed any professional code of ethics.

Nevertheless, the subject of laws to govern counseling sparks debate among some Christian and pastoral counselors who say, God is their only authority. Others acknowledge the right of a state to protect the health and welfare of its citizens, yet many fear future encroachment of the laws that might limit Biblical counseling approaches. As we believe, Scripture always brings a balance to the issue.

The Bible reminds the people to be subject to rulers and authorities, unless it subjects them contrary to Scripture, to be obedient, and to be ready to do whatever is good, to slander no one, to be peaceable and considerate, and to show true humility toward all men. (Titus 3:1-2)[90]

Following that advice keeps us in compliance with almost any law regulating ethical counseling practice.

The Christian and secular counselor organizations have codes of ethics that detail what is considered ethical practice for members. When you accept membership in or certification from an organization, you are affirming your intent to follow the prescribed code of ethics. If you do not, you face censure and expulsion from the organization and withdrawal of your certification.

Conclusion

You must take time to read the code of ethics for any organization in which you seek membership. Codes of ethics generally take a position on the nature of the therapist-client relationship, the proper uses of appraisal instruments, humane standards for research, the prohibition on dual relationships, standards for private practice, and the appropriate conduct in the consulting relationship. In addition to those positions, codes of ethics for Christian counseling associations include a statement of faith and confirm the appropriate use of biblical authority as an element in the counseling process.

Most organizations include their code of ethics in their new-member packet. One should review several statements as part of one's decision making process before committing to membership in any Christian or secular organization. The combination of the Bible and the code of ethics bring to bear every law of God and man to help the counselor make the right choices. Some well-defined examples of secular codes of ethics are those from the National Board of Certified Counselors, the American Counseling Association, and the American Psychological Association. For Christ-centered codes of ethics one should review the positions of Christian Associations for Psychological Studies, the American Association of Pastoral Counselors, and the American Association of Christian Counselors.

Introduction to Children and Adolescence

There has been a growing awareness in the past decade of the impact of substance abuse, with the establishing of MADD (Mothers Against Drunk Driving), SADD (Students Against Drunk Driving), DARE, involving school children's awareness of drugs, etc. The full picture includes data reflecting the number of individuals and family members who are adversely affected by substance abuse.

Some have described group psychotherapy as a vehicle for removing the roadblocks that so often keep us from getting past our own pain. Caution and special attention should be used by any therapist involved in helping a client remove any roadblocks, allowing them an opening in getting to the heart of the matter.

Many people believe that dynamically oriented group work cannot be done with alcoholics, but it was Dr. Vannicelli and her colleagues, in their work that have given considerable thought to trying to understand both the origins of this view as described in their book (Vannicelli, Removing the Roadblocks, 1992), and the source of its perpetuation (Vannicelli, Dillavou, and Caplin, 1988). From this side of the psychiatric community, one can well imagine that some bias may have grown out of frustrations and negative experiences as well as from practitioners who attempted to use traditional therapy on alcoholic patients who continued to drink.

The bias on the part of dynamically oriented caregivers is not uncommon today. What is most interesting about this is that it is common even among therapists who do attempt to use dynamically oriented therapy with other self-destructive, crisis-prone population e.g., adolescent or suicidal patients. Some positive results have been gained.

Chapter XXV
The Multi-Method Approach

Many practitioners have avoided the use of group settings because of the seemingly perception that the interaction of a group as a whole would somehow interfere with the members' individual goals.

Improved group assessment has attempted to upgrade this perception, with allowing the group to provide each person with a major source of feedback about the behaviors that are annoying or pleasing to others, and the opportunity to respond regarding these cognitions.

One important aspect of this approach allows the group leader to use a number of therapeutic procedures that are unavailable or less efficient in the therapeutic dyad. Among these procedures is group reinforcement, which for many children is more powerful than individual reinforcement. Group methods can provide models of behavior by using, and monitoring the results. In addition, the group provides a natural laboratory for learning discussion and leadership skills that are important to good social relationships.

One can identify at least four general categories of coping skills commonly pursued in multimethod groups: interpersonal, problem-solving, cognitive, affective coping, and self-management. All of these are aimed, either directly or indirectly, toward specific problematic situations. Achievement of these skills mediates the attainment of specific treatment goals designed for each individual in the group. Each of these general skill categories in terms of its relevance to the multimethod group-treatment approach is presented.

1. Interpersonal skills are critical for healthy development in children. Interpersonal skills have been defined as those responses which, within a given situation, prove effective or, in other words, maximize the probability of producing, maintaining

or enhancing positive effects for the interactor. As a result of increased interpersonal skills development, a child's social status may change. In this area, the group leader can assist the children in assuming leadership roles, allowing them to demonstrate a wide range of skills, not previously observed by their age-mates.

2. Intervention aimed at developing problem-solving skills has been increasingly applied to child and adolescent problems. This application has been spearheaded by Spivack and Shure's work on assessment and teaching of interpersonal cognitive problem-solving skills (ICPS) to children (Spivack, Platt and Shure; Spivack and Shure, 1974).

Problem-solving skills can maximize a child's adjustment and interpersonal effectiveness.

Cognitions refer to thoughts, images, thinking patterns, self-statements, or private or convert events that may be inferred from verbal or other overt behavior.

Cognitive coping skills are not, however, the only coping techniques available for dealing with problematic or stressful events.

Problem-solving, social and cognitive skills can all be regarded as coping skills. One of the most useful coping skills is the ability to relax in stressful situations. If children can respond to stressful stimuli by relaxing, they will be better able to access other coping skills. Furthermore, once relaxation is mastered, it may enhance a child's or adolescent's general quality of life.

Self-management is another important skill. This refers to those procedures through which children control their own environment as a means of controlling their own behavior by using environmental cues, self-monitoring, self-instructions, self-evaluation, and self-reinforcement. Although the data supporting the use of any one of these procedures is limited in scope, there is clinical evidence that these procedures may be effective following the use of more direct environmental strategies (Stuart, 1977). In any case, the child will still be struggling with various problems long after the group has terminated and can utilize these learned skills even when only limited external support is available.

The Various Methods as presented by Sheldon Rose and Jeffrey Edledon are:

The Problem-Solving method, which involves learning and carrying out a systematic set of steps for solving a problem (Heppner, 1978).

The modeling sequence method is designed to teach specific positive interactive behaviors and includes such techniques as overt modeling, behavior rehearsal, coaching, and group feedback.

Cognitive change methods involve the children being trained in more effective ways of evaluating themselves or problematic situations.

Relaxation methods are taught to children who need help in coping with stress, pain, anger, or external environmental events in which no external coping behavior is possible.

The socio-recreational method involves the use of active games, board games, arts, crafts, storytelling, and dramatics to facilitate the achievements of therapeutic goals and to increase group cohesion.

The effective use of these procedures may be more important than the particular strategy being utilized.

The major phases in moving forward with the multimethod group approach are; planning for group treatment, orientation of the client and significant others to the possibilities and limitations of group treatment, assessment of the presenting problems, the client resources, interventions to effect change, and generalization of that change to the real world. These phases are guided by the group leader rather than evolving naturally out of the group. They are somewhat overlapping in time and in content. Each phase implies a different emphasis for the group leader.[91]

Chapter XXVI
Planning Family Treatment and Orientation

Planning in advance is a very important characteristic of the multi-method approach of counseling. Areas of planning include; putting the group together, arranging a series of meetings, deciding on the focus of each separate meeting, selecting treatment procedures, and planning for transfer or generalization. This planning should not be haphazard, but rather, it should be based on the best available information collected from parents and teachers, children in the pre-group interview, ongoing observations and contacts with the children and significant others throughout group treatment. It also draws on data from empirical studies. The plan should not be a rigid structure that can never be departed from, but rather a well-thought-out point of departure on which to base preparation and ongoing decision making. It provides a basis for explaining to the parents and their children what the group is all about and how it will proceed. Groups are then selected, and the type of group decided from the number of children, and the determined need.

Prior to treatment, the group leader usually interviews each child, and depending on the resources of the agency and on the referral source, the parents, teacher, supervisor, parole officer, or other significant person in the child's life.[92]

Chapter XXVII
Assessing Children's Problems

The major purposes of assessment in small-group treatment are to formulate the presenting problems to determine whether a child can utilize a small treatment group to resolve the problem(s), to ascertain what kind of group can best serve him or her, to identify individual and group plans of intervention, to evaluate whether ongoing treatment is having an impact or whether the completed treatment was effective, and finally, to contribute to knowledge about the parameters of the treatment strategies in general. To achieve these purposes, problems presented by the children, their parents, or teachers are formulated together with the children in terms of concrete overt and covert behavior, as it occurs in a specified situational context.

Through the focus of the pre-group interviews and the early group sessions on assessment, it is a process that continues throughout the treatment. Initially, determining and selecting the appropriate group and individual target problems are the focuses of assessment. Later, continuing assessment is used to facilitate decision making. Finally, assessment shifts to evaluating the ongoing progress and outcome of the individuals and the group.

There are many ways in which children can be trained to identify specific behavioral responses to situations. Training in behavioral specificity can be carried out through group exercises. The children are presented with case studies in which the behavioral responses of problematic situations are described in general terms or character attributes, such as, "When Irvin is asked by his mother to help with the dishes, he becomes lazy." or "When Tina doesn't get to do what she wants to do, she gets mad." The children are then asked to reformulate the responses in terms observable behaviors. Another training opportunity occurs when the children describe situations from their diaries. Group members are encouraged to evaluate the response descriptions in terms of specificity as well as to evaluate the appropriateness of the response.[93]

Chapter XXVIII
Changing Behavior

Modeling procedures lend themselves especially well to the group-treatment setting. A group contains an abundance of potential models; new models can be introduced without seriously disrupting existing social patterns; and multi-person role-playing can be readily utilized. The effective use of modeling procedures depends upon several factors. These include the child's skill to observe and imitate others, special attractive attributes of the model, similarity of the model to the client in various personal characteristics, the way in which the model is presented, and the incentives under which the modeling and subsequent imitations take place (Bandura, 1975).

There are basically two approaches to modeling: unstructured and structured. The most common unstructured approach is to bring the group members into contact with desirable models and hope for the best. This can be structured slightly by telling the models which behavior to demonstrate while in the group. The most common structured procedure is through role-played modeling in the group meeting. Pre-structured videotape, skills, and puppet shows are other ways of demonstrating the model's characteristics to the audience.

In order to change behaviors, various types of consequences must be considered in group treatment. These could include; social reinforcement, activities as reinforcements, token reinforcement, group contingencies, material reinforcement, time-out from reinforcement, response cost, and punishment. These are all powerful tools in the modification of behavior when used properly.[94]

Chapter XXIX
Helping Children Cope

The most common cognitive procedure used with young children, both individually and in groups, is self-instructional training. This procedure has recently gained wide support from clinicians as well as researchers. However, its clinical application has, thus far, out-stripped its research support (Cormier and Cormier, 1985).[95]

Self-instructional training has generally been used with children characterized by high frequency of hyperactive, aggressive, and impulsive behavior. It has been used to develop skills in such areas as resistance to temptation, delay of gratification, problem solving, reading, and creativity.

In the phase of test analysis, the group leader attempts to ferret out common critical moments in the problem situation that seem to interfere with the performance of the task.

As we move into cognitive modeling, the group leader or experienced group member models the various self-instructional training points internally while explaining aloud what is happening in the situation. Following the modeling and discussion, the group leader introduces cognitive rehearsal. Cognitive rehearsal is the role-played practice by the members of the same situation simulated by the model. It is possible for each child to perform a task with another member performing the role of the group leader. This arrangement provides additional practice in a short period of time.

As we move from the thinking out loud phase, we move into what is referred to as fading. Fading prepares the children to instruct themselves privately. The first step in the process of fading is for the children to rehearse whispering the self-instructions as the group leader describes what is happening. Since the whispering is not too intrusive, it is possible for all the children to whisper at the same time. However, some group leaders prefer to carry out this phase in pairs with one pair monitoring the whispering of the other and providing feedback to the other. The whispering step may be modeled by the group leader, or by a member who seems to understand the process.

The group is an efficient means of providing a rationale for each of the procedures used. A number of group exercises are helpful to children in identifying self-defeating statements and to learn self-reinforcement. Relaxation can also be taught readily in groups, and group members can improve their relaxation skills by relaxing each other.[96]

Chapter XXX
Using Games and Activities

Reviewing and development of homework, modeling, rehearsal, feedback, exercise, problem solving, group discussion, practicing relaxation, and cognitive restructuring are all part of using games to achieve goals. Depending on how it is presented, much of what is done can be fun to the children.

The purposes of these activities are multiple. First, they are used to increase the attraction of the group in the early phase of treatment. Second, they create a variety of problematic or stressful situations in which the members can reveal and/or practice their coping skills. Choosing roles, selecting activities, losing a game, failing to complete a task, meeting demands for cooperation, and requests to clean up are all situations that may require new behaviors, such as assertion, humor, interviewing, problem solving, self-organization, and decision making. The group leader uses these situations to reinforce effective coping, to assess coping strengths and deficiencies, and to try out new skills. The leader also monitors the use of newly learned skills and coaches their use in the ongoing process. Third, group activities provide a variety of new roles and leadership opportunities for members. These roles can be coached during the group process and rehearsed, either as homework or in the treatment part of a group meeting. This is one of the few opportunities for many clients to be helpers of others, a star player in a given sport, or a coach, and to fill other attractive social positions that may not be available to them in the normal classroom situation. Finally, group activities provide a rich opportunity for direct observation of children interacting with one another under various stress levels. It can become a major source of observed behavioral data for assessment and evaluation.

Activities are analyzed in terms of the physical field, the required behaviors, and the informal behaviors associated with it. The physical field refers to the minimal physical space, materials, and equipment required to carry out a given activity. Often the group meeting room is quite circumscribed. It usually is a small classroom or a lounge. The materials available can control and enhance the skill training in specific ways. The availability of tools makes certain programs possible. Access to a television or film camera opens up a wide range of activities. Various kinds of sports equipment and crafts supplies all expand the nature of what can be done in the group. Another aspect of physical field is the time required for a given activity. Often a session can have as little as five to ten minutes available for an activity, including the instructions. It would be difficult to carry out most activities in such a limited time without modification of the rules. Some games, however, can be squeezed into a short time period, carried over to another session, or completed as a homework assignment.

The constituent behaviors are those behaviors that are essential to a given activity and are required of the participants. Game-playing, behaviors such as rolling dice, moving a piece one space at a time, and taking turns in the same order are examples of constituent performances.

Informal behaviors are associated with but not essential to the performance of a given activity.

Many types of activities are used in group treatment. Some of these include games, such as, sports, action, paper and pencil, card, board, and social skill. Handicrafts, drawing, charades and dramatics, simulated classroom activities, photography, and field trips are also used. Games provide an opportunity for the occurrence of such behaviors as taking turns, giving feedback, following rules, and learning how to lose and how to win. Most games are highly prescriptive, but the control is lodged in the rules rather than with the group leader. The game format is especially useful with disruptive and resistant adolescents.

Although they rarely show initial interest in the work of the groups the adolescents are often swept up in an exciting game.

By identifying a number of game categories one can facilitate planning and decision making in the selection of game activities. One of the most commonly used games with pre-adolescents is Capture the Handkerchief. In this game two teams with the same number of members are selected by the group leader. Each member of one team is given a number, and duplicate numbers are given to members of the other team. The group leader stands between the teams and holds a handkerchief aloft. While calling one of more numbers, the group leader drops the handkerchief. The children with the assigned numbers run up to the handkerchief. The object is to grab the handkerchief and get back to one's own side before being tagged by the person with the same number on the opposite team. A point is given for either getting back to one's own side safely or tagging one's opponent with the handkerchief.

Often, art activities are used to increase manual dexterity and spontaneity. They are usually characterized by a low level of physical movement and inter activeness unless the group leader designs the activity to increase physical movement and interaction among members. For children who become anxious when interacting, arts are an ideal starting point, with the gradual addition of interactive activities, such as subgroup or group projects. The group can combine crafts with other activities such as, laying out, and coloring the prototype of a social-skills board game, or making scenery for a play. This is not the only use of dramatics. For many children with few social skills, game skills, or crafts skills, dramatics is often a means to accrue status in the group or at least to take pleasure in a leisure-time activity.

Charades are often used as a preparation for putting on skits or for eventually rehearsing behaviors. However, they are also an important activity in their own right with both children and adolescents.

On occasion, field trips should be considered for practicing newly learned skills in the real world and ample reinforcement for a wide variety of roles and behaviors. These excursions involve group planning, decision making, cooperative behaviors, obtaining information, and teaching others. Because of the great popularity of excursions, they are often used as group contingencies for continued assignment completion.

Making decisions about program activities may be an excellent way for members to try out newly learned decision making skills. But if decision-making skills are generally deficient or weakly developed in the group, planning may be so chaotic that members will have an aversive experience without ever deciding on an activity. Therefore, until the point that rudimentary decision-making skills are developed, program activity decisions remain largely in the hands of the group leader. At the same time, however, the leader gradually shapes decision-making skills. For example, the children might first choose between two possible activities described by the group leader, such as volleyball or kickball, or between two types of field trips. Successful decision making by the group at this level may lead to more open choices at subsequent meetings. When children and adolescents make choices, they, too, must take into consideration treatment goals just as the group does.

If the program activity is well prepared and meets the interests of group members, the members are usually highly satisfied with them. This alone does not imply that program activities are sufficient to correct specific behavioral problems. It is an important and necessary tool, along with social-skill strategies, cognitive restructuring, and general patterns. Activities take place in the group environment. They serve the interest of the group and are served by them.

The concept of group structure and group process has been proposed as a means of systematical analyzing group phenomena. Group structure refers to the various patterns of group interaction at a given point in time. Group process refers to these patterns of structural change over time. Group structures include, group norms that govern interaction, role structure in which specified behaviors are attributed to certain positions of categories of persons in the group, patterns of interpersonal liking or group cohesion, and patterns of interpersonal communication. All of these structural concepts have been used extensively to analyze the group and its relation to member's satisfaction and group productivity. Group processes include the patterns of change of norms, roles, cohesion, and other group structures. Other examples of group process might include changes in the intensity of anger or other affective responses over time, changes in the intensity and relevance of mutual self-disclosure, and changes in the degree of task orientation of instruction.[97]

Chapter XXXI
Assigning New Behavior

It is possible to view the entire treatment process as preparation for carrying out the assignments for practicing new behavior outside of the group. Subsequent meetings may be used to evaluate the effectiveness with which the assignments were performed. In fact, a portion of almost every session is devoted to the monitoring of earlier assignments and the design of new ones.

Once children have been prepared to deal with the problem in the real world through role playing, reinforcement, and other group procedures, they should design a plan to implement these newly learned behaviors or cognitions in the real world. The carrying out of this plan may be regarded as the implementation phase of the problem-solving process. Reporting back to the group or a buddy is the verification phase of the process.

One major purpose of assigning homework in the treatment process is to encourage the children to try out in the real world what they have learned in the group. A second purpose is to provide members with the opportunity to try out new behaviors in the absence of both the group leader and the pressure of the group's immediate feedback. It is also a method of helping the children to become the principal agent of their own change and to decrease their dependence on the group as the major source of help. A third purpose is that homework permits treatment access to private behaviors, such as sleeping disorders, sexual disturbances, or private thoughts that would not be available in the group context. A fourth purpose is, in the absence of the group and leader support the child is often forced to develop self-control strategies to comply with the homework requirements. Finally, an important goal of assignments is to provide an opportunity for multiple trials beyond the limits of the group.

Often in the group, because of limited time available in a session, only a few role-plays can be carried out by each person. Homework provides an opportunity for continued and repeated practice.

Different kinds of assignments may be used, each of which deserves separate examination, are interactive tasks, cognitive restructuring tasks, observational tasks, and non-interactive tasks, including observation of self and others, and reading assignments.

Interactive tasks are assignments in which the child talks with others outside the group in highly specific ways. In general, these tasks are observable social phenomena with limited boundaries in terms of time, place and action. Cognitive restructuring tasks involve examining and changing self-talk associated with stressful or problematic solutions. An example may be an adolescent who is about to have a job interview. His task is to covertly instruct himself to relax, to take one step at a time, and to remind himself that he really does know the job for which he is applying.

Often cognitive restructuring and interactive tasks are combined. One example where this might occur is when the adolescent is preparing for the job interview by using self-enhancing self-talk. He also has to perform the actual verbal task of carrying out the interview.

Since cognitive assignments are difficult to monitor, only self-report at subsequent meetings or contracts with buddies is used to monitor whether the assignment was completed. With children, concrete reinforcement of cognitive or other non-monitorable assignments is unadvisable.

Simulated tasks are special cases of interactive tasks. They differ in that the behavior performed in the real world is role-played interaction rather than an actual interaction with a significant other. In self-observational assignments, clients observe their own behavior, cognitions, or feelings in specific situations and record them.

It is not sufficient to merely give assignments. The clients must comply with the assignments if the desired effects are to be achieved. A number of strategies have been established to maximize the probability of compliance.

Clients should be well versed in specific details of the assignment if they are to complete it. That is, each group member should know when the assignment is to be carried out, with whom, under what conditions, what behaviors or cognitions are to be implemented, and if and how the results are to be monitored and reported back to the group.

Adequate preparation is necessary to assure the client is aware of how to carry out the assignment. If the client is unsure how to carry out the assignment, additional rehearsal may be necessary. If the assignment is successfully completed the individual should be reinforced by either something in the environment when the assignment is performed or by the group at a meeting when the client reports on the success. In addition, the clients should covertly reinforce themselves for the performance of the assignment at the time of the performance.

In most groups, assignments are put into writing at the end of the meeting and signed by both the group member and the group leader or buddy. Written assignments, if calling for explicit rewards or contingencies following successful completion, are called contingency contracts.

Initially, it is difficult for children to remember what they must do in a given assignment and when it is to occur even if heavy reinforcement is used. To this end, the group leader uses a variety of cueing strategies to remind the client when and what is to happen. Initial assignments should be relatively easy to perform, but subsequent assignments should gradually increase in difficulty and complexity as they gradually approximate the treatment goal.

The group leader should initially help each client to develop as many external monitoring sources as possible. Later such monitoring sources should be phased out and only self-report should be used.

Maximum involvement in the selection and planning for an assignment is another way of increasing the client's private commitment to the effective performance of that assignment. Initially children and adolescents do not have the basic skills to design their own assignments. Thus, the group leader plays a major role in planning assignments in the first few sessions of treatment, carefully taking into consideration the child's interests, which the leader will have determined in pre-group interviews and in prior group discussions.

As noted, maximum involvement increases private commitment to completion of the contract. The client should be encouraged to make a public commitment to the group and eventually to the immediate social circle on which the assignments impinge. In situations where a client's cognitive distortions seem to be preventing the client from completing the assignment, cognitive restructuring strategies should be used.

Not all the work of the group can and should occur within the group session. It should always be remembered that assignments are useful only if they are completed. Treatment without extra-group assignments, though possible, appears to reduce the power of the entire treatment process. Extra-group assignments such as modeling, reinforcements, and cognitive restructuring, are the major strategy in implementing transfers of change to the real world.

Transferring changes from the group setting to the natural environment begins with agendas that incorporate the following principles: increasing members' responsibility for their own treatment; providing multiple and varied situations for members to practice with; simulating the real world in the training context; preparing for the unexpected, for a hostile environment, and for potential setbacks; overtraining members in the desired target behavior and cognitions; training in conceptualizing specific experiences and in mediating generalization; and directly instructing members in practicing generalization.

The transfer of group leadership behaviors and intervention skills from the group leader to the members increases the members' responsibility. The group leader begins to train and delegate treatment planning activities, modeling, feedback, problem solving, discussion leading, and decision making as early as possible in the treatment process, increasing members' responsibilities at each successive session. Discussion leading, though important, is not the only leadership activity in which group members are trained and for which they assume responsibility. They are trained in skills required to plan their own group program, to help other members to design their own assignments, to deliver reinforcements to each other, to model appropriate behaviors to each other, to provide information for each other, and so forth. Once these and other leadership skills are learned, the group leader creates opportunities for and encourages the members to carry out these behaviors themselves. A successful performance of leadership behaviors is initially followed by verbal reinforcement.[98]

Chapter XXXII
The Bible and Adolescence

The concept of adolescence, as we know it, did not appear in the literature on child-rearing until late in the nineteenth century. It was not until 1904 that the term adolescence was first used by Dr. G. Stanley Hall, the first president of the American Psychological Association.[99]

With this historical background it should come as no surprise that the word adolescence does not appear in the Bible. The biblical writers probably did not think of adolescence as a separate period of human development. Childhood, on the other hand, was mentioned with some frequency and the fact that instructions are given directly to children would imply that these children were old enough to understand and comply. Biblical teachings on children, therefore, undoubtedly apply to "children" of adolescent age.

The Bible also speaks to "young men" and "young women". The writer of Ecclesiastes, for example, tells young men to rejoice:

Young men, it's wonderful to be young! Enjoy every minute of it! Do all you want to; take in everything, but realize that you must account to God for everything you do. So banish grief and pain, but remember that youth, with a whole life before it, can make serious mistakes.[100]

Young people are portrayed in Scripture as visionaries who are strong, able to incorporate the word of God into their heart and mind, to overcome Satan, are expected to be submissive to elders, told to love their mates and instructed to humble themselves "under the mighty hand of God, that He may exalt you at the proper time, casting all your anxiety on Him, because He cares for you".[101] These few phrases give considerable guidance to adolescents and, of course, the teachings of the entire Bible can be helpful to young people struggling with adolescence, just as the Scriptures are helpful to those who are older.

Conclusion

Perhaps the most difficult task involved in counseling children and adolescents is to establish a trusting relationship and to help the counselee recognize the need for help. Some pre-adolescents and adolescents will come voluntarily for help, but often they see no need for counseling and are sent by a parent, teacher, or judge. In such cases the counselor may be seen as the parents' ally and resistance can come out from the beginning. Honesty and respect, mixed with compassion and gentle firmness, can be the best point to begin adolescent counseling. You may find resistance, if so, deal with it directly and give the young person opportunity for self-expression.

The counselor must recognize that he will often be treated with hostility, suspicion, fear, or praise primarily because of the counselor's appearance or position which resembles some other adult. This should be discussed with the client, observing and discussing the attitude toward the counselor can be of value.

It is very difficult to help if you cannot indentify the problem, and since adolescents sometimes deny that they have problems, the counselor is in a challenging position. Instead of trying to classify or diagnose the young person's difficulties, it is helpful to encourage both pre-adolescents and adolescents to talk about such issues as school, leisure activities, home, parents, religion, plans for the future, dating, sex, likes and dislikes, worries, and similar issues, starting with relatively non-threatening items. Some general questioning may be needed to get the process started, but once the young person starts to talk, the counselor must be alert in his listening. Once you begin to identify the problems, there is value in determining what you want to accomplish in counseling.

Family counseling is a great approach to counseling, in which the entire family is seen together. This approach allows the family to work together in a group setting, as a family. The group approach works especially well when the group members have problems with interpersonal relations, a tendency to withdraw, or a problem which each of the members have in common, or share, such as alcoholic parents or a terminally ill relative. The relationships that are built in such counseling sessions can give support and teach the children an important lesson, how to relate to others effectively.[102]

Introduction to Counseling into the Next Century

With-in this new century, Christian Counseling will likely see some very important changes as we move forward into the next century, and not the least of these changes is getting back to the Bible as a solid standard, and our final authority for basic life principles and truths.

As we continue into the next century it is becoming more and more apparent that Christian counseling is far more than a ministry, a profession or a business, it is truly a calling! As such, at the beginning of any endeavor, regarding Christian counseling, it is well to be reminded that Holy Scripture reminds us to examine the motives of our hearts.

Education, experience, specialized training, and time comprise the inventory of any counseling center. Counseling skills alone are not enough to sustain inept management. Good Christian counseling center managers must be good workers, but not all good workers make good managers. As the profession/calling progresses, someone must fill the complex role of counselor/administrator. This role will demand much in a daily mix of counseling, setting appointments, preparing reports, bookkeeping, and even, at times, making coffee. Without the assistance of the Holy Spirit and the understanding of the call into Christian counseling, the demands may become too great.

As the government becomes more involved in attempting to regulate our profession, the risk will be ever increasing. The only risk free guarantee you get in this life is the security of salvation after accepting Christ as your personal Savior, and Him accepting you into His family, and assuming the call to service, for the sake of our Lord Jesus and His Gospel, and a willingness to help His people.

Chapter XXXIII
Counseling into the Next Century

State or Church oversite in the calling/ministry of pastoral care and counseling is the question that should be the consideration of licensure in this century, and this will surely become very prominent as we move forward. Many Christian practitioners will become more involved in treating people's "mental" problems, much the same way as other practitioners of mental health are perceived as treating people's mental problems. The question of licensure in this framework of reference will attempt to consider whether or not pastoral/Christian counselors should be licensed by the state in order to practice counseling and psychotherapy and to deal with questions of mental health. But, we must ask, what should the state have to do with the licensing of ministries of the church? And, conversely, and a much better question is, what should be the responsibility of the church in overseeing its own ministries?

Other questions and discussion to be considered into this century will be:

Whether or not it is legitimate or appropriate for the state to license persons as pastoral counselors. Would it be too restrictive in view of the separation of church and state as required by the First Amendment of the Constitution;

The appropriateness of state licensing beyond the already existing religious authorization of the ministry; and

Whether or not the religious authorization to practice within the ministry can be extended to include the concept of licensing counselors or the use of counseling methods within a religious framework.

"...However strong the state's interest in universal compulsory education, it is by no means absolute to the exclusion or subordination of all other interests." [103]

Clearly the debate will continue with tests to try to balance the quality of belief's against the strength of the state's interest, not permitting the state to claim any form of controlling interest over the church. The importance of the free exercise clause to Christian counselors is the bar that it represents to the state using mental health issues as a means of restricting the practice of Christian counseling. This will become an even greater issue as we continue to move deeper into the next century.[104]

Bibliography

Paul D. Meier, M.D., Frank B. Minirth, M.D., Frank B. Winchern, Ph. D., *Introduction to Psychology*; Baker Book House (1983)

Perry London, *The Modes and Morals of Psychotherapy*; New York: Holt, Rinehart and Winston (1984)

Jay Adams, *The Christian Counselor's Manual*; Baker Book House (1983)

Richard Gene Arno, Ph.D., Phyllis Jean Arno, Ph.D., *Creation Therapy*; The Sarasota Academy of Christian Counseling (1993)

The Living Bible

The Holy Bible; KJV

William H. VanHoose and Jeffrey A. Kottler; *Ethical and Legal Issues in Counseling and Psychotherapy*; Jossey-Bass Inc. (1985)

Robert Henley Woody and Associates: *The Law and the Practice of Human Services*; Jossey-Bass Inc. (1984)

Taber's Cyclopedic Medical Dictionary, F.A. Davis Company, Philadelphia, PA (1968)

Joseph Adelson; *Adolescence and the Generalization Gap*; Psychology Today (Feb. 1979)

Sheldon Rose, Jeffry Edleson; *Working with Children and Adolescents in Groups*; Jossey-Bass (1987)

Cormier and Cormier (1985)

J. Demos and V. Demos; *Adolescence in Historical Perspective*; Journal of Marriage and Family 31 (1961)

Gary Collings, Ph.D. *Christian Counseling: A Comprehensive Guide*; World Books (1980)

Samuel H. Kraines and Eloise S. Thetford; *Help for the Depressed*; Springfield, IL; Charles C. Thomas (1972)

Rene Spitz; *Annalistic Depression*; the Psychoanalytic

Aaron T. Beck; *Depression: Causes and Treatment*; Philadelphia; University of Pennsylvania Press (1967)

Ian Gotlib and Catherine Colby; *Treatment of Depression*; Pergamon Press (1987)

Gregory W. Brock and Charles Barnard; *Procedures in Marriage and Family Therapy*; Allyn and Bacon (1992)

William J. Bennett; *The Index of Leading Cultural Indicators*, Published by Empower America-The Heritage Foundation-Free Congress Foundation (1993)

Endnotes

1 Paul D. Meier, M.D., Frank B. Minirth, M.D., Frank B. Winchern, Ph. D.; *Introduction to Psychology*: Baker Book House, pg. 307-310.

2 *Holy Bible NIV* (1 John 1:9) (Phil. 3:13-14) (Rom, 12:2) (1 Thess. 5:14)

3 Perry London, *The Modes and Morals of Psychotherapy* (New York: Holt, Rinehart and Winston. (1964), pg.32.

4 Ibid. pg. 10.

5 Jay Adams, *The Christian Manual* (Baker Book House, 1983), pg.71-72.

6 Richard Gene Arno, Ph.D. Phyllis Jean Arno, Ph.D.; *Creation Therapy*; Published by; The Sarasota Academy of Christian Counseling (1993) pg. vi.

7 Ibid. pg. vi-vii.

8 *Holy Bible KJV* (Hebrews 4:12)

9 *Holy Bible KJV* (1 Thessalonians 5:23)

10 *Taber's Cyclopedic Medical Dictionary*, F, A, Davis Company, Philadelphia, PA (1968).

11 *Holy Bible KJV* (2 Corinthians 5:17)

12 Jay Adams, *Christian Counselor's Manual*; Baker Book House, (1983) pg. 98.

13 *Holy Bible NIV*, (Ephesians 5:15)

14 *Holy Bible NIV*, (Colossians 4:5, 6)

15 Gary Collins, *Christian Counseling: A Comprehensive Guide*, World Books (1980) pg. 29.

16 *Holy Bible NIV*, (James 2:17)

17 *Holy Bible NIV*, (Hebrews 11:6)

18 *Holy Bible NIV*, (Matthew 11:28-30)

19 *Holy Bible NIV*, (Isaiah 53:3)

20 *Holy Bible NIV*, (John 1:10)

21 *Holy Bible NIV*, (Matt. 27:46)

22 *Holy Bible NIV*, (Matt. 5:44-45)

23 Paul D. Meier, M.D., Frank B. Minirch, M.D., Frank B. Wichern, Ph.D.; *Introduction to Psychology & Counseling*; Published by: Baker Book House (1983) pg. 260-261.

24 Jay Adams; *The Christian Counselor's Manual*; Published by: Baker Book House (1983) pg. 380.

25 Paul D. Meier, M.D., Frank B. Minirth, M.D., Frank B. Wichern, Ph. D.; *Introduction to Psychology and Counseling*; Baker Book House (1983) pg. 261.

26 Samuel H. Kraines and Eloise S. Thetford; *Help for the Depressed*; Springfield, IL; Charles C. Thomas (1972) pg. 44.

27 Rene Spitz; *Anaclitic Depression: The Psychoanalytic Study of the Child*; (1946) pg. 313-342.

28 Roger Barrett, *Depression: What It Is and What to Do about It*; (Elgin, IL. David C. Cook, (1977) pg. 32.

29 Gary Collins, Ph.D.; *Christian Counseling*; World Books (1980).

30 Aaron T. Beck; *Depression; Causes and Treatment*; Philadelphia; University of Pennsylvania Press (1967) pg. 255.

31 *Holy Bible NIV*, (Psalm 43)

32 *Holy Bible NIV*, (Job 3; Num. 11:10-15; John 4:1-3; Exod. 6:9; Matt. 26:75)

33 *Holy Bible NIV*, (1 Kings 19:4)

34 *Holy Bible NIV*, (Matt. 26:37-38)

35 *Holy Bible NIV*, (Romans 15:13)

36 Ian Gotlib and Catherine Colby; *Treatment of Depression: An Interpersonal Approach*; Pergaman Press (1987) pg. 43, 45, 47, 58.

37 Ibid. pg. 62, 63, 64, 71, 72, 73, 76, 77, 83, 84, and 94.1, 72, 73, 76, 77, 83, 84, and 94.

38 Ibid. pg. 91, 96, 99, 104, 116, 117, 118, 139, and 145.

39 *Holy Bible NIV*, (Philippians 4:10-19)

40 *Holy Bible NIV*, (Ephesians 5:22-32)

41 Gregory W. Brock, Charles Barnard; *Procedures in Marriage and Family*

Therapy; Allyn and Bacon; (1992) pg. 6, 7, 8, 9, 10, 11, 12, 14, 15, 18, 21, 22, 27, 29, 33, 34, 35, 37, 39, 40, 4`, 41, 42, 45, 55, 56.

42 Gregory Brock and Charles Barnard; *Procedures in Marriage and Family Therapy*; Allyn and Bacon (1992) pg. 57, 58, 59, 65, 67, 68.

43 Gregory Brock and Charles Barnard; *Procedures in Marriage and Family Therapy*; Allyn and Bacon (1992) pg. 69, 73, 74, 75, 76, 77, 78, 79, 80, 83, 84, 85, 86, 87, 88, 90, 91, 95, 100, 104, 105, 106, 107, 123, 126.

44 Ibid. pg.129, 130, 131, 133, 134, 135, 138, 191.

45 *Holy Bible NIV*, (1 Corinthians 13)

46 *Holy Bible NIV*, (Romans 5:5-8)

47 *Holy Bible NIV*, (Proverbs 13:24)

48 *Holy Bible NIV*, (Deuteronomy 6:5)

49 *Holy Bible NIV*, (John 13:34-35)

50 *Holy Bible NIV*, (1 John 3:23)

51 *Holy Bible NIV*, (John 14:21)

52 *Holy Bible NIV*, (Ephesians 5:25-30)

53 *Holy Bible NIV*, (Proverbs 22:6)

54 *Holy Bible NIV*, (Proverbs 23:13-14)

55 *Holy Bible NIV*, (1Timothy 3:4-5)

56 Paul D. Meier, M.D., Frank B. Minirth, M.D., Frank B. Wichern, Ph. D.; *Introduction to Psychology and Counseling*; Baker Book House (1983) pg. 377-380.

57 *Holy Bible NIV*, (Ephesians5:23)

58 *Holy Bible NIV*, (Mark 10:45)

59 *Holy Bible NIV*, (Matthew 11:29; Philippians 2:5-8)

60 *Holy Bible NIV*, (Genesis 2:18)

61 *Holy Bible NIV*, (Exodus 18:4, Deuteronomy 33:7, Psalms 70:5, Hosea 13:9)

62 *Holy Bible NIV*, (Genesis 3:16)

63 *Holy Bible NIV*, (Colossians 3:18)

64 *Holy Bible NIV*, (Ephesians 5:21)

65 *Holy Bible NIV*, (1 Peter 3:7)

66 *Holy Bible NIV*, (Romans 12:1)

67 *Holy Bible KJV*, (Psalms 139:13-16)

68 William J. Bennett, *The Index of Leading Cultural Indicators*, (Published Jointly by; Empower America, The Heritage Foundation, and Free Congress Foundation, March 1993)

69 Ibid.

70 Meier, M.D., M., Minirth, M.D., Winchern Ph. D.; *Introduction to Psychology and Counseling*; Published by: Baker Book House, 1983, pg. 22 and 111.

71 Ibid. pg. 155.

72 Ibid. pg. 298.

73 Ibid. pg. 299-300.

74 Ibid. pg. 301.

75 Ibid. pg. 301-302.

76 Ibid. pg. 302-303.

77 Ibid. pg. 303.

78 Ibid. pg. 303-304.

79 Ibid. pg. 304.

80 Ibid. pg. 304-305.

81 Ibid. pg. 309.

82 William H. VanHoose and Jeffrey A. Kottler; *Ethical and Legal Issues in Counseling and Psychotherapy*: Josey-Bass Inc. (1985) pg. 1, 2, 3, 5.

83 Ibid. pg. 9, 10, 11, 13, 15, 18, 20, 21, 23, 24, 25, 31, 32, 33, 34, 38, 40, 42, 43.

84 Ibid. pg. 44, 45, 46, 47, 48, 49, 54, 56, 60, 61, 62, 63, 67, 68, 69, 71, 72, 75, 77, 79, 80, 81, 84, 85, 86, 87, 88, 89, 90, 92, 93, 94, 95, 96, 97, 98, 99, 100, 107.

85 Ibid. pg. 108, 144, 145, 146, 147, 153, 156, 159.

86 Ibid. pg.163, 168, 169, 170.

87 Robert Henley Woody and Associates; *The Law and the Practice of Human Services*; Jossey-Bass; (1984) pg. 113, 114, 115, 117, 118, 119, 121, 122, 123, 127, 129, 131, 139, 141, 143, 146, 150, 151, 153.

88 Ibid. pg. 289, 290, 292, 292, 293, 295, 296, 297, 298, 299, 307, 309, 313, 319, 324, 330, 331, 335, 337.

89 Ibid. pg. 373, 376, 377, 380, 384, 385, 386, 387, 393, 395, 400, 401.

90 *Holy Bible NIV*, (Titus 3:1-2)

91 Sheldon Rose, Jeffrey Edleson; *Working with Children and Adolescents in Groups*; Jossey-Bass Publishers (1987) pg. 6-22.

92 Ibid. pg. 29, 40.

93 Ibid. pg. 61-62, 72, 76-77.

94 Ibid. pg. 147-148, 154-155, 182.

95 Cormier and Cormier (1985)

96 Rose and Edleson, pg. 208, 213, 214.

97 Ibid. pg. 239, 240, 242, 243, 248, 249, 251, 258, 260, 263, 264, 266, 273, 275, 276.

98 Ibid. pg. 310, 311, 312, 313, 314, 315, 316, 317, 318, 319, 320, 322, 323, 324, 327.

99 J. Demos and V. Demos, *Adolescence in Historical Perspective*, Journal of Marriage and Family 31 (1969) pg. 632-638.

100 *Holy Bible LB*, (Ecclesiastes 11:9, 10)

101 *Holy Bible NIV*, (Acts 2:17; Prov. 20:29; Jn. 2:13-14; Titus 2:4; 1 Peter 5:5-7)

102 Gary Collins, Ph. D.; *Christian Counseling: A Comprehensive Guide;* World Books (1980) pg. 229-231.

103 Yoder, (Supra) pg. 215.

104 Ibid.